# Arrogance on Campus

# Lewis B. Mayhew

# ARROGANCE ON CAMPUS

Jossey-Bass Inc., Publishers
615 Montgomery Street • San Francisco • 1970

ARROGANCE ON CAMPUS
by Lewis B. Mayhew

**Copyright © 1970 by Jossey-Bass, Inc., Publishers**

*Jossey-Bass, Inc., Publishers*
*615 Montgomery Street*
*San Francisco, California 94111*

**Library of Congress Catalog Card Number 71-128699**

**International Standard Book Number ISBN 0-87589-074-1**

Manufactured in the United States of America
   *Composed and printed by York Composition Company, Inc.*
   *Bound by Chas. H. Bohn & Co., Inc.*


JACKET DESIGN BY WILLI BAUM, SAN FRANCISCO




FIRST EDITION

*Code 7026*

# THE JOSSEY-BASS SERIES IN HIGHER EDUCATION

*General Editors*

JOSEPH AXELROD, *San Francisco State College
and University of California, Berkeley*

MERVIN B. FREEDMAN, *San Francisco State College
and Wright Institute, Berkeley*

# *Preface*

*rrogance on Campus* is the result of an attempt to understand the variety of crises which engulfed American college and university campuses during the second half of the 1960s. It deals in paradox for it seeks to answer why to one broad question: During a period in American higher education when more students were being educated by the most highly trained and best paid faculty of any time in history, when more public support was provided, when the term *educator* achieved high regard, when more financial support was provided students, indeed when higher education was succeeding beyond the wildest expectations of earlier periods—why campus disruption?

# Preface

Although I have made a serious attempt to analyze objectively and with some perspective, I am also a part of the scene and experienced deep feelings when my own institution was torn by a sequence of upheavals. The original completed manuscript was in the hands of the publisher when the events of April and May 1970 shook not only the campuses but the national fabric as well. Time is required to put those events in perspective. Yet so germane to the rest of the book were they that a final chapter dealing with them seemed mandated. Thus that chapter and the others which precede it reflect feeling as well as, hopefully, thought.

In much of *Arrogance on Campus* blame is placed and judgments are made. Sharp criticism is made of certain tendencies within faculties, student bodies, and central administrations. This criticism is made deliberately in the belief, first, that error can be corrected if identified and, second, that unless error is corrected, the potential power and influence of higher education for public good could be destroyed. Although *Arrogance on Campus* does deal with categories of people—faculty, protesting students—it also deals with abstractions and seeks to derive from them design for reform. Thus power is accepted, as are tension and conflict, and ways are sought to use power and conflict for creative and healthy ends. Although the book is critical, some may even say destructive, of academic policies and values, it is nonetheless based on an abiding faith in freedom and education. It argues only that abuse of freedoms will bring about their demise.

In a sense *Arrogance on Campus* is also prophetic in the sorts of remedies it proposes; these remedies do run counter to conventional wisdom. Thus, it argues that while students should be heard and their educational needs should be met, they have no inalienable right to participate in academic governance. Furthermore, it sees that presidential power is essential for stable governance but that a sufficient base of power has eroded. This condition can be rectified only through restoration of power and authority to central administration. And *Arrogance on Campus* is conservative in the sense that the authors of the Federalist Papers were conservative. It accepts the possibility of human error and seeks to

# Preface

minimize its impact through constitutionalism and a system of checks and balances.

Although the tone of *Arrogance on Campus* could be called angry, my feelings are fundamentally hopeful. Arrogance on campus has produced much damage. Faculty members too frequently have placed their own interests above those of their students. Institutions and their leaders have been insensitive to profound social change. And a serious backlash to higher education has developed. But reform is still possible, as some institutions have demonstrated. I hope *Arrogance on Campus* points to some fruitful ways for others to reform themselves.

In the hope for a better future, this work is dedicated to my wife, Dorothy C. Mayhew, who tolerated my essential travel, survived my gloom, which arrogance on campus produced, and encouraged my faith that people can change their institutions for the better.

*Stanford, California*
*September 1970*

LEWIS B. MAYHEW

# Contents

# Contents

# Arrogance on Campus

# Arrogance on Campus

*A* major part of campus unrest during the last half of the 1960s can be best explained as the result of arrogance. Professors, students, administrators, and board members acted arrogantly and without due concern for the rights and beliefs of others. Out of arrogance came confrontation, which when escalated led to violence, repression, and a threat to public as well as to academic order.

American higher education has accomplished more in a shorter time than any educational system in history. Since World War II it has accommodated unprecedented and unexpected numbers of students, increased the training of its faculty, and rewarded its faculty better—doubling salaries between 1958 and 1970. It has intensified the rigor of the education it offers and has also proved that university independence and federal support of research can be combined, in at least some fields, to produce needed new knowledge and theory. And higher education is moving toward achievement of a national goal of making higher education available to every child in every state.

Higher education has made these advances through the efforts of many different people and as a result of many different forces. College presidents have secured funds, provided buildings, and searched out qualified faculty. State legislators have provided the finances to double or quadruple institutional budgets in less than a decade. Students and their parents have indicated general approval, by students attending in ever larger numbers and by students' and their parents' paying an ever larger share of the cost. Board members and presidents, once thought to represent the greatest threat to academic freedom, have become so enlightened and sophisticated about such matters that academic freedom is no longer in danger from forces within the higher education community.

But higher education is in as grave a position as at any time in its history. At the very crest of its power and regard it is bringing severe reaction from parents, donors, legislators, congressmen, the business community, the downtrodden, and even its recent graduates. This crisis is brought about by many factors—failure to achieve perfection, imbalances in program development, crescendoing of other social ills needing support, and failure to respond quickly enough to new demands which were placed on higher education out of confidence in its powers. But a central factor in precipitating the troubled times higher education is experiencing

2

are the waves of unrest, protest, and violence which have convulsed colleges and universities since 1964. Much if not most of student protest could, in the past, be attributed to institutional vulnerability, lack of provisions to safeguard student procedural rights, and sheer administrative ineptitude. But those problems are rapidly being solved, and the protests, violence, and rejection of rationality continue. Hence, other explanations must now be sought to explain why a president of Cornell was in trouble because he acted with caution and mercy and why a president of Harvard was criticized for using force to calm similar sorts of turbulence.

Make no mistake as to the gravity of this crisis. If campus disorders do not end, the political establishment will assume control of colleges and universities, and higher education will lose its freedom, which is the acme of its past achievements. Hopefully, higher education will be able to place its own house in order, but to do so the forces of disruption and violence must be honestly faced and carefully examined, even when that examination, like this one, is painful.

Campus unrest and student militance can in part be interpreted as a struggle for power between adversary and antagonistic groups. But the identification of adversaries and their differences have been generally misunderstood. Militant, protesting, and sometimes nihilistic students, whose proportion among all students is small but whose influence is disproportionately large, claim that the administrations and boards of trustees are the villains, that conditions would improve if faculty and students could only have the power to govern jointly.

However, the faculty, epitomized by a minority, of which I may well be one, is the real enemy of students. The administration has sought to contrive the relevant, exciting, innovative education students claim to desire, while college faculty members have generally been resistant to educational change and innovation; such change threatens a style of life and interests they have found congenial. Admired and well-paid professors in prestigious institutions have gained the right to set their own goals, determine their own activities, and assess their own performances. Increasingly, if con-

3

ditions warrant, they do not include teaching in these activities, or they restrict their teaching to the few who are willing disciples. Senior professors who have escaped teaching undergraduates protest, perhaps too much, that they like to teach but that the system or their own work just does not allow it. Junior faculty meanwhile seek to teach graduate students and to get on with their work. And faculty members, acting alone or in unison through departments, have limited the power of the administration to make needed educational reforms. Much of the trouble at San Francisco State College in 1968 and 1969 arose because departments controlled all positions and denied the president the power to appoint people to work with black admissions and black studies.

Although the threads of campus unrest are varied, involving structural flaws, frequently excessive size, and imperfect planning, one essential is the coexistence of arrogant groups, such as the faculty, each pursuing its interests and goals to the detriment of all others. Militant, protesting, radical, or nihilistic students form another of these groups and act out of an arrogance which, were it not so destructive, could almost be called sublime. This arrogance in its several forms has its roots in a complex of causes. So although fault may be found and blame assigned, it should be with an awareness of and a sympathy for this background. An affluent society has led those who share it to expect instant satisfaction and has stimulated rage in those who do not. Rapid technological change has left the young bewildered and uncertain about the future. Television has altered how people perceive reality, but they are still also indoctrinated by older styles of communication. The indelible scar from the Depression has given the adult population preoccupations incomprehensible to those born after World War II. And the equally indelible scar from slavery and racism has generated guilt in the majority white population and insistent demands for long overdue rectification in the black community. Then, too, there are the war, the threat of atomic destruction, and the uneasy realization that perhaps Marx was right in believing that a capitalistic society can survive only as a war based economy.

A small group of students presume to have the wisdom to

4

make and to have others accept immediate moral judgments about these critical issues. They proclaim that the war in Viet Nam is contrary to fundamental morality or natural law (as they perceive it). They place corporations, which supply the goods and services the government requires in pursuing a national policy arrived at through legitimate means, beyond the pale of moral respectability. Their concept of morality also does not include military service to a society organized as a nation-state. However, many of us who served in World War II and participated in the invasion of Europe feel we are still moral men. Students who attempt to stop a university from doing defense work do not inquire whether participation in defense work has ever been justified and if so with what differences. University-developed radar saved England in World War II, and the proximity fuse, also developed through university research, shortened that war. A judgment can be made that the war in Viet Nam represents an unfortunate initial decision, implemented with excessive means, for results which are not worth the high cost of life and treasure and that it should be ended as quickly as possible without jeopardizing essential national needs. But each element in that judgment represents more than uninformed and inexperienced moral indignation.

To defend these questionable moral judgments, the militant few feel justified in imposing their will upon all others. Denying a student the right to be interviewed by a legitimate enterprise, whether it be the CIA, Dow Chemical Company, or the Marine Corps, is denying civil rights through a minority and nonlegitimate decision and is no more defensible than is denying admission to college on the basis of race. Protesting students, of course, claim that the system (rarely defined) is so rotten that only through such acts can they dramatize the immorality of war. Or, the more sophisticated say that since ideational confrontation is the business of the university, even illegal confrontation is appropriate. But this is casuistry. Of all recent confrontations, only the civil rights movement in the South can be defended because the political and judicial systems did not provide avenues for remedying centuries of abuse of Negroes.

5

## Arrogance on Campus

The militant and alienated students, once again a small minority, also assume the right to stand in judgment of those who lead, without ever having had the awesome experience of making truly responsible decisions which affect others. Each person and each generation are fallible. But anyone who has not had to decide whether to drop an atomic bomb, when to send troops to certain death, how to invest university funds, or even whether to make the quarter million dollar investment which is a tenure appointment is not in a position to stand in judgment. The young see, often with blazing insight, the failings of their parents or teachers. A drunken father, an illiterate mother, or an inarticulate professor is none to be emulated. But these each have been on a road youth yet must travel, and until it has passed those miles, it is not yet privileged.

An unfortunate manifestation of youthful arrogance is youthful impatience. Militant youth wants, or at least says it wants, instant truth, instant justice, instant reorganization of an enterprise which has taken eight hundred years to build. In part the blame may rest with their elders who have argued an apocalyptic thesis. But the concept can still be criticized. The young people at Harvard or Stanford in 1969 were protesting matters which already were in the process of resolution; ROTC would go eventually at Harvard, just as the Stanford Research Institute would eventually be reorganized. But the impatience of youth certainly focused attention on the issue and on the institution and, in the process, probably cost each institution five to ten million dollars. To put the morality issue in perspective, five million dollars would have provided full scholarship for four years for three to four hundred disadvantaged students at a time when Stanford and Harvard both were searching for funds for minority group members. Universities have been reluctant to change, but they have. The impatience of youth for more rapid change than the system can tolerate has resulted in the election of Ronald Reagan, legislative outrage throughout the country, and a backlash which may set higher education back fifty years.

One of the frightening arrogances of this minority of students is their rejection of rationality. Their embracing of the mystical folk ideal of pure feeling and emotion is indeed sinister to one who saw what reliance on folk traditions did to German youth in the 1920s and 1930s. They believe that if faith can be put in participatory democracy, in the goodwill of the common people (whom students do not like—witness hatred of police, who are working people)', and in the race, all will be well. This view flies in the face of the long struggle between rationalism and the jungle. If man has a unique role, it is to exercise his reason and to make conscious choices. But the militant young say, "Feel! Feel! Feel!" just as German youth said, *"Blut! Blut! Blut!"* Modern man is still too much a child of Aristotle to reject feeling. But feeling is the twin power of cognition, which also should be put to the service of the organism. To reject reason is to reject reality. And this the militant young sometimes seem to do.

This is a harsh indictment but similarly strong comments may be made about some faculty. Faculties, like any other large subculture, contain many people with different interests and attitudes. But a number, and they are too frequently found in the posts of universities, display an arrogance which flavors faculties generally and serves as the real adversary to the healthy aspirations of youth. Still the minority on which blame is being placed are not totally responsible. Society has tempted faculty members by expecting them to fill new roles for which their tradition provided no guidance. It has asked them to accept overwhelming numbers of students without helping them to understand why they should. For too long it undervalued and underpaid its teachers, which in part explains their acquisitiveness once conditions changed. And institutions have too long been administrator centered, with faculty members frequently considered as mere employees. But once again, lethal traits must be exposed if ultimate cure is to be attempted. To begin, there is the arrogance of presuming that what interests a faculty member should be of concern to all others. Faculty members were generally highly intelligent children who gained greater satisfaction in solitary activities than they did in groups. As they grew older their interest in something—science, reading, rocks—deepened, and in college they became preoccupied with their subject. Eventually,

7

sometime after receiving the bachelor's degree, they realized that college teaching was the only vocation which would support their continued interest. And as college teachers, they are in a position to argue that no one can be truly educated who does not speak German, know the restoration dramatists, understand plant ecology, or appreciate the Civil War and Reconstruction period. This arrogance has resulted in overburdened curricula and excessive graduation requirements.

This tendency would not be so hurtful were it not for the arrogance of intellectual preciousness. Most blatantly this preciousness is reflected in the classics professor who simply cannot countenance offering the classics in translation; the psychologist who, in spite of student requests, does not allow a course in the psychology of adjustment because it currently is not in vogue; or the sociologist who can tell an aspiring social worker that since sociology as taught at that institution is not concerned with people but with theory, sociology is an inappropriate base for future social work. Preciousness generally is just irksome, but in faculty members it blinds to the serious problems which currently face a modern university. The intellectually precious just cannot be bothered to find literature which speaks to the recently enrolled disadvantaged Negro in an idiom he can use and with a theme to which he can relate. The result, of course, is one more dropout.

Equally destructive is the arrogance of behaviorism or, properly more pejoratively, scientism. American professors have so embraced behaviorism and quantification that philosophers no longer question, theologians accept the death of God, and sociologists prefer the graph to the reality of a community. Those brave few who do attempt to interpret life broadly are scorned as popularizers or journalists. Even in the humanities, the motives of artists are treated with more time and care than are the works themselves. And words such as *enjoy, feel, appreciate* no longer are respectable for the scientistic humanist. Students ask seriously for help in understanding themselves and are told to read experimental studies statistically significant but of vast unimportance.

There also is the matter of research. In agriculture, engineer-

8

ing, physics, biology, and medicine some professors in American universities have accomplished much. But the number actively engaged in significant research in even the greatest of research oriented universities is painfully small. Ten thousand new journals would be needed if each American professor made the modest contribution of one scholarly paper a year. Yet research is so overwhelming that faculty members generally demand and expect reduced teaching loads and ponderously proclaim that teaching and research are inextricably entwined and that the production of knowledge is the essential role of the university. The one posted office hour a week is intended to imply that the professor has more important things to do than to see students.

Another arrogance is the belief of faculty members that they can govern the university in addition to performing their other duties. Faculty should be involved in governance, but those who make important decisions about allocation of funds, building priorities, tuition, admissions, and public relations without spending the requisite time to assimilate information and reflect on alternatives are arrogant. A modern university is a complex organization requiring highly specialized people to make critical decisions. Yet the faculty senator, who would be the first to criticize a generalist or popularizer in his field, meets for a dozen hours, skims reports, and votes to abolish a sixty million dollar research installation or discredit a president's handling of student uprisings. With such amateur governance, no wonder the universities seem poorly managed.

The success of the academic revolution has brought a new kind of arrogance, that of consulting with those in political or financial power. There is something heady about flying to Washington weekly to consult with federal authorities or to New York to serve on the board of Standard Oil. Somehow the opportunity to serve on a panel which will approve millions in research contracts seems much more important than just teaching students. And the interesting paradox is that professors, who claim to disdain men of business or of bureaucracy, nonetheless eagerly await the call to advise them. Eric Goldman could wait neither to serve President

Johnson nor to write a somewhat vindictive account of the man he saw as the philistine from Texas.

Administrators and trustees have also exhibited a share of arrogance, although the more extreme forms took place in the past. Presidents have acted capriciously in matters affecting students and faculty. Boards have sought to oust faculty members on the basis of rumor and have tried to impose the business model on a university structure. And administrators have tended to be overly secretive, believing that they alone possess discretion.

But the encounter between faculty and student arrogance seems most involved in campus turmoil. The dynamics by which these two arrogant groups manage to bring institutions to a halt are relatively easy to perceive. Faculty members attend to their own work, forcing students into classes either taught by the inexperienced or dealing with the professors' most recent intellectual concerns (sometimes recency, of course, means the Ph.D. thesis of twenty years earlier). Students in such a situation feel alienated and frustrated and come to believe that no one cares for them. They then search for an outlet for their feelings of unease and generally strike out at cafeterias, residence halls, or other manifestations of institutional life. But if student leadership is smart (and increasingly it is), it searches for institutional vulnerability, a not too difficult undertaking. Once students have seen racism in admissions, institutional violation of due process, or a tainted institutional connection with the CIA, they make the attack. At this point central administration is paralyzed, not because the illegality of a sit-in, arson, or destruction of records is not clear but because the president cannot know whose side until then the lethargic faculty will take. If he moves to the civil authorities, the faculty weeps, ostensibly for students bullied by a police state, but actually because the police threaten syndicalism. If the administration waits until faculty uneasiness finally turns to a desire for tranquility, it loses the confidence of parents, donors, and those upon whom the institution depends for survival. In 1969 the president of Harvard called civil authorities, the president of Stanford did not. Neither was the right decision because there can be no right decision when dealing with the fruits

10

of raw arrogance. Sooner or later order is restored, and since the university is a hardy thing, it resumes serving society. Generally, some changes are made; some are wise and well in process before the episode, and some, which likely do not last long, are made entirely under pressure as a price for survival.

This is a bleak picture, but it is still possible and honest to end this analysis on an optimistic or creative note. Within America, a distinct civilization of which in spite of its failures we should be proud, several powerful ideas even now are beginning to restore balance and order. First, there is the eighteenth century concept of the perfectibility of man. This concept alone could but lead to frustration; but when coupled with the second, equally important element, pragmatism, it does lead to impressive achievement. For example, the central city was once thought to be doomed to deterioration as the concentric rings of suburbs expanded, but now it can be as magnificent as the central part of Atlanta. Again, various groups in the society have from time to time been considered uneducable. But gradually the poor, the Irish, the agricultural and mechanic classes have been educated and have joined the mainstream of American life, and the Negro has finally joined their ranks.

Third, there is the materialism noted by many from de Tocqueville down to the most recent flower child. Materialism has been decried as an evil of American civilization, but it produced a Marshall plan, a Point Four program, even a Peace Corps, in which the young were ministering not to the souls of people in developing countries but to their very real material needs. In this sense materialism is the very spirit of the Christian and Jewish religions. Jesus did not ask, "Did you go to church? Did you observe the fast days?" Rather, He asked, "Did you visit the sick, feed the poor, shelter the homeless?" (in short, attend to material needs). How can this materialism affect the crisis of the campus? Order has returned to troubled campuses because the large majority of antagonists finally realized that continued violence jeopardized preparation for a job, for marriage, and for children, and a chance to share in the benefits which American productive power has made possible.

The fourth idea is that of constitutionalism as a way of handling controversy and of bringing about social change at a rate society can tolerate. Constitutionalism accepts the reality of power, of conflicting desires and interests, and of the corruptibility of absolute power; it provides, through checks and balances and through specified processes, ways by which these conflicting forces can be accommodated. Earlier the university community was reluctant to accept these differences; the ideal of the romantic rural community was too strong. But the unbridled display of power seen recently on college campuses has revealed the need for constitutions, bylaws, and ensured due process. As these are established, as surely they will be, justice and tranquility will return to the campus.

# CHAPTER I

*Impasse and Interpretation*

It would be a mistake to view arrogance as the result just of human perversity. Militant, protesting students are that way for many reasons, highly important among which is the disparity between the liberal values on which they have been nurtured and in which they believe and the facts of large

13

and impersonal bureaucracies. Indeed the worst features of student dissent reflect liberal tendencies grown malignant and lethal.

College students, who are young and human and who are trying to establish their own identities, are and always will be a mystery and a problem to their mentors. Young Italian students in the thirteenth century caused faculty members, whom they employed, so much trouble and frustration that faculty members asked the civil authorities to take over the operation of the university. Eventually the civil authorities created a lay board of trustees to do the job. In Paris in the thirteenth and fourteenth centuries students wrote dirty stories on church walls, disrupted oral examinations, threw garbage on passersby, and physically harmed professors. In nineteenth century America students shot at professors, protested a draft law, beat up participants in a meeting of which they did not approve, and went on violent strikes about the quality of food. And in the twentieth century American college students vowed never to fight for their country, supported a foreign and presumably communist power in Spain, drank illegal liquor, and experimented with sex. No understanding of present student demands and protests is possible without awareness that tension between students and their society is part of a most human condition.

But perhaps student activism and student demands today are qualitatively different from those at other times. If this is so, the difference must derive from radically different conditions, for the human being has changed little in the eight hundred years since the University of Paris opened its doors. Obviously, conditions always change. Paris was different from Bologna, which in turn faced different situations from those at Berlin, Oxford, or Harvard. However, since World War II the world, and in a magnified way the United States, has faced the largest number of revolutionary changes in history. The revolt of colonial peoples has challenged traditional ideas as to who shall be educated and who governed. The weapons revolution has barred victorious war as an aim of public policy, but nations have not evolved criteria even for declaring a limited war. The technological revolution has made affluence possible for people in advanced nations and through the

**14**

revolution in media has made possible contrasts of that largess with the poverty of people in less developed nations. This technological and cybernetic revolution has also eliminated the need for thousands of people in the work force, thus forcing the young to search for activities to occupy their time until adult society is ready for them. American society especially has experienced the revolution of urbanism but is attempting to cope with it through the techniques and strategies of a rural and agrarian age. Many academic rules were made to deal with fifteen- and sixteen-year-old farm or village children, away from home for the first time. These rules cannot be applied to city youth in their early twenties who have already tasted complete personal freedom. But the greatest revolution is the revolution in rate of change; many of the vocations needed in the year 2000 are as yet unknown and unnamed. Youth in college are vaguely aware that they are traveling toward an unknown station.

The issues involving students must be viewed and eventually resolved in this context. The troubles facing the campuses will not be eased by applying instruments appropriate before the revolutionary decades of the 1950s and 1960s. Telling nonwhites to stay in their place, restricting to campus twenty-five-year-old violators of late hours regulations, or having students anticipate a future role their counselors do not even know of will not work. Treating all students and student-raised issues in the same way also is not realistic. As educational opportunities have expanded, colleges and universities have attracted populations almost as heterogeneous as the nation itself. There are many ways of classifying students—on ability; on whether they are academically, socially, or vocationally oriented; or on several of many dimensions of personality or character. But since this is an inquiry into pathology, perhaps a typology of problems or issues would be the most helpful.

Most visible and vocal is the 2 to 5 per cent of the student body who can be described as militant, revolutionary, and even nihilistic. These young people believe that the society is so sick it can never recover. They feel intensely the ambiguities and inconsistencies in the society and complain about a democratic nation in which people starve, about a country of immense natural beauty being spoiled by commercial interests, about a nation dedicated to peace acting imperially, and about a people so satiated with goods that alcoholic, televised, or drugged sedation alone will help to pass the weary hours. This militant group, well exemplified by the SDS, place their faith in feeling, participatory democracy, and the basic goodness of the working man. They see vividly the evil workings of the industrial-military-educational complex. These students, convinced of the inevitability of revolution, provoke confrontations over the most trivial matters in the hope that acts of violence will bring reaction which can then ignite further conflagration. This group is perplexing because its members are generally intelligent children from relatively comfortable and liberal homes who have finally found their security and reason for being in their movement. This group is particularly dangerous because its members believe in and even use the same idiom as have several other generations in conflict with an adult society which has lost its legitimacy. Protesting German youth in 1814 defeated constitutionalism, thus paving the way for Prussian militarism. Russian militants in the 1890s killed the czar and destroyed Russian constitutionalism, which eventually precipitated the Communist revolution. Militant Serbian students planned and executed the assassination of Archduke Franz Ferdinand, which ignited the conflagration of World War I. And militant youth, in protest against their elders in Germany in the 1920s for having lost the war, welcomed Hitler as the personification of the revolutionary ideal. The phrasing of a young American is vicious in its premises, reminiscent of the rhetoric of older revolutionary movements, but probing in its insight:

> American society, because of its Western-Christian-capitalist bag, is organized on the fundamental premise that man is bad, society evil, and that people must be motivated and forced by external reward and punishment. We are a new generation, species, race. We are bred on affluence, turned on by drugs, at home in our bodies, and excited by the future and its possibilities. Everything for us is an experience, done for love or not done at all. We live off the fat of society. Our fathers worked all year round for a two-week vacation. Our entire life is a vacation! Every moment, every day we decide what we are going to do. We do not

16

groove with Christianity, the idea that people go to heaven after they are dead. We want HEAVEN NOW! We do not believe in studying to obtain degrees in school. Degrees and grades are like money and credit, good only for burning. There is a war going on in the Western world: a war of genocide by the old against the young. The economy is closed. It does not need us. Everything is built. So the purpose of universities is to get us off the streets. Schools are baby-sitting agencies. The purpose of the Vietnam war is to get rid of blacks. They are a nuisance. America got the work she needed out of blacks, but now she has no use for them. It is a psychological war. The old say, "We want you to die for us." The old send the young to die for the old. Our response? Draft-card burning and draft-dodging! We won't die for you.[1]

Although in 1969 there seemed to be a rapprochement between militant protesting white students and Negroes, it would be a mistake to confuse the two groups or to treat them and their problems as one. Negro youth has occupied buildings; presented institutions with ultimata to grant black power, black studies, and separatism or burn; destroyed property in bookstores and cafeterias; and even contributed to the heart attacks of several presidents. And as the numbers of Negro students increase on college campuses, as they must, these acts of outrage and violence are likely to increase at least for a time. Negro youth have experienced the success of the civil rights movement and have learned workable tactics from it. They have seen how, in spite of impressive political gains, the economic, social, and educational achievements have not been gains but losses. They recognize the pervasive racism built into even the most innocent social instruments, such as access to higher education. Given a chance they are going to end racism or use racism to gain the things which they rightfully desire. Thus, they stress blackness, black beauty, and black studies, saying that through them they will find their way to full black manhood. To attempt to oppose such demands with logic, historical example, or coercion will do no good. Eldridge Cleaver reveals this search for manhood in violent ways in his comments about Watts:

[1] J. Rubin, "A Yippie Manifesto." *Evergreen,* May 1969.

17

"Baby," he said, "they walking in fours and kicking in doors; dropping reds and busting heads; drinking wine and committing crime; shooting and looting; high-siding and low-riding; setting fires and slashing tires; turning over cars and burning down bars; making Parker mad and making me glad; putting an end to that 'go slow' crap and putting sweet Watts on the map—my black ass is in Folsom this morning but my black heart is in Watts!" Tears of joy were rolling from his eyes.

It was a cleansing, revolutionary laugh we all shared, something we have not often had occasion for.

Watts was a place of shame. We used to use Watts as an epithet in much the same way as city boys used "country" as a term of derision. To deride one as a "lame," who did not know what was happening (a rustic bumpkin), the "in-crowd" of the time from L.A. would bring a cat down by saying that he had just left Watts, that he ought to go back to Watts until he had learned what was happening, or that he had just stolen enough money to move out of Watts and was already trying to play a cool part. But now, blacks are seen in Folsom saying, "I'm from Watts, Baby!"—whether true or no, but I think their meaning is clear. Confession: I, too, have participated in this game, saying, I'm *proud* of it, the tired lamentations of Whitney Young, Roy Wilkins, and The Preacher notwithstanding.[2]

Another problem group in addition to the activists and the militant blacks is that large group of alienated or uncommitted who are inclined to drop out of the mainstream of American life in favor or drugs or the hippie culture, or simply to a less achievement oriented level of society. They find an industrial urban setting too complex, human motives too devious, and symbols of achievement —martinis before dinner, mink capes, and too powerful automobiles —not worth the effort; so they search for tranquility and simplicity. The ideal life says one is "getting back to the land and finding out how to live off the land, how to make our own clothes, grow our own food, how to live as a tribal unit."[3] And about education we have this clear message from a twenty-one-year-old ex-college stu-

[2] E. Cleaver, *Soul on Ice* (New York: Dell, 1968), p. 27.
[3] N. Van Hoffman, *We Are the People Our Parents Warned Us Against* (Chicago: Quadrangle, 1968), p. 137.

dent and heavy drug user: "University is great, man, sure is nice all the things you can learn there. But it's too bad that you're supposed to go there and learn there things so that you'll forget them the next day. And that's generally what it's for. You know the university is a test. You make it through the university and you get your grade, and then you go with your grade and somebody pays you to do something."[4]

Although the etiology of the college dropout, hippie, or drug user reflects great variety, a common theme is a critical adolescent identity crisis manifested in regressive and ineffectual behavior, which obscures some quite positive, searching aspects of the rebelliousness. Frequently a set of family problems predisposes the individual to opting out—parental unauthenticity, despair, or ambivalence about success and achievement. At the same time these problems predispose adults to react by trying to isolate, stereotype, and punish the dropout.[5] A good example is this case of a drug user in the Haight Ashbury district in San Francisco:

> The boy's father is a doctor; [the boy has a] high IQ, [is] bright, but [is] resentful of his younger sisters, and [is] a very fat boy. This boy's rebellion took a passive form. You could make him go to school, but you couldn't make him learn. Therapy was unsuccessful. Then he began to shoot up, and as he grew taller he slimmed down, which brought him into a phase of his life when he'd hang around Sunset Strip and smoke grass. He played the defy-the-fuzz game with the other kids without getting busted, but finally he did—for walking across the street on a yellow light. They found pills on him, but they were legitimate ones for hay fever. Next he ran away from home and was taken in by a couple of waitresses who didn't know he was only fifteen. He lived *ménage à trois* with them, and meanwhile he learned about acid—took it two or three times—and then learned about pimping. Finally he got busted. The cops found marijuana on him and the court said he was incorrigible. His family sent him

[4] J. T. Carey, *The College Drug Scene* (Englewood Cliffs, N.J.: Prentice-Hall, 1968), p. 15.

[5] E. A. Levenson, "Socio-Cultural Issues." In L. A. Pervin and others (Eds.), *The College Dropout* (Princeton, N.J.: Princeton University Press, 1966).

19

East to school and that lasted two or three months, when he broke the conditions of his parole and ran away to the Haight. That's where I found him and took him with me to Oklahoma City, where we sent him to summer school. I believe the thing he likes about me is that I know more about pot than he does. Altogether he's taken acid thirty to forty times in the last two and a half years. Before he took acid his IQ tested at 140. Two and a half years later he retested at 112. That's one way of looking at what happened to him; but he's much less anxious than he was, more relaxed, more concerned with the pleasures of the moment. He reminds me of teen-agers I've examined who've had frontal lobotomies, but how much of the damage is reversible if there's been biological scarring is uncertain. Today this boy likes himself better. You have to realize that lobotomies make people happy; they attenuate those inner struggles and conflicts that are characteristic of the human condition.[6]

The large majority of students do not protest, drop out, or place extreme demands on institutions; nevertheless they must also be viewed as an unresolved issue. This majority has the power to bring an institution to a halt when its needs are too flagrantly ignored or its collective conscience is outraged. At Berkeley, Columbia, and Stanford initial confrontation between a small group of activist students and the institution escalated because the majority became concerned about something—free speech, police brutality, or double jeopardy. To understand why these students, seemingly content with college, can be so quickly converted into an irresistible pressure group, it is necessary to understand something of their developmental needs as human beings and to realize that little in the college experience seems designed to meet these needs. College students seek ways to extend or expand their impulse life in order to use their powers of affection or emotion. And the college serves them disciplined rationality. They demand freedom to explore in ways consistent to them and are inclined to decry the rat race of prerequisites and too many courses. And the colleges give them more. Although they get their greatest satisfactions from the peer group and are searching for ways to make themselves independent

[6] Van Hoffman, *op. cit.*, pp. 234–235.

20

of their families, they nonetheless search for adequate and appropriate adult role models with whom to identify or to test their emerging personal identity. All too frequently professors just are not around enough to meet this need. Perhaps the most common student goal is self-understanding and awareness of their own identities. They sense that to have self-understanding they must have group identification and powerful ways of relating intimately with other people. But they are inclined to use social and athletic activities as better devices for this personal development than the formal curriculum or intimate contact with very many teachers. Thus, when students' needs are unmet, they generally contrive other ways of satisfying them.

The college years are tension-ridden and anxiety-laden, but this majority of students do not feel this situation to be especially debilitating. They recognize the pain of conflict and like assistance on their terms in resolving it; they do not judge this conflict as catastrophic. But it can be if the desired help is not offered. Thus, underlying distress over unavailability of professors becomes converted to a massive protest over defense related research. In addition, students do not generally view the college curriculum as being particularly pertinent to them; and they do not judge it retrospectively as having made much contribution to their personal development. This vague feeling of the majority of students that their education is not very good is the nerve which, when touched by a specific episode, reacts in sometimes violent and generally unpredictable ways.

Two other factors in this volatile equation need to be exposed. The first is the matter of students' personal rights. Although regional differences do exist, this generation of college students has generally been reared in permissive homes and been allowed great personal freedom. Then they enter college and find their hours, clothes, and personal habits restricted for reasons they cannot comprehend; disenchantment sets in. If these restrictions are coupled, as they so often are, with arbitrary or autocratic decisions made by administrative officers and professors, a syndrome of discontent evolves. Frequently the syndrome is mild and is expressed in demands for parietal rights, equal rules for men and women, the right to have cars, and some strengthening of student control of residence halls. But it also may be far-reaching and include demands for freedom from all university control over all nonacademic behavior, with the implication that the student should deal only with the civil authorities over the use of alcohol or drugs, possession of firearms, and the like. Institutions, of course, deal with these matters in different ways. Their responses range from the complete openness at some of the prestige private institutions, which take the position that what a student does out of class is completely his own business, to regulations of dress, forms of recreation, study hours, and language. The University of Rochester only proscribes active firearms on campus and does not condone the use of illegal drugs, while Wheaton College still requires the Wheaton pledge, proscribing dancing, card-playing, smoking, and attending movies. But the demands for freedom are surely spreading, and they create significant friction between the student and his institution.

The second factor is the pathological reaction of adults to these various forms and manifestations of student unrest. The conservative backlash to student unrest is reflected in legislative attempts to mandate law and order; administration overreadiness to use police power or to ban certain speakers, books, or activities; and trustee attempts to remove faculty or administrative prerogatives. The situation in California exemplifies much of this reaction, with a governor who would like to intervene in private institutions if he thought he could and who can, in all seriousness, suggest bayonets as appropriate means for ensuring institutional tranquility. Such a stance is pathological because it simply intensifies trouble rather than diminishing it. Several California institutions have been the scenes of escalated conflict because of the use of vindictive measures which elicited fresh outbursts from students and increased the proportion of students engaged in protest. Possibly Nixon's publicized praise of the hard line Father Theodore Hesburgh took at Notre Dame was not unrelated to the spate of student outbursts later that spring.

Another pathological adult response to student disturbances, made by some aging professors and theorists, is that youth is always right and that even violence is generally justified because the system has so mistreated youth. Such individuals may be highly respected scholars who to their own work apply the most rigorous criticism; but they tolerate inconceivably loose thinking in youth on the ground that since youthful sentiments are so pure, their ideas are valid. Paul Goodman affirms this view.

> At present in the United States students—middle class youth—are the major exploited class. (Negroes, small farmers, the aged are rather outcast groups; their labor is not needed and they are not wanted.) The labor of intelligent youth is needed, and they are accordingly subject to tight scheduling, speed-up, and other factory methods. Then it is not surprising if they organize their own CIO. It is frivolous to tell them to go elsewhere if they don't like the rules, for they have no choice but to go to college, and one factory is like another.[7]

The tragedy comes, of course, when students believe such statements.

Obviously these troubles must be overcome, and the distressing conditions on college campuses must be improved. Equally obviously the leadership in the society—presidents, board members, political leaders, parents—must do the responding. But the response had better be made with full understanding and with creative goals and objectives in mind. Youth in each of the categories discussed demonstrate highly objectionable behavior and have hurtful attitudes. But they also have some of the highest ideals and exhibit the most commendable comportment. Both tendencies must be faced because in these difficult times a resolution must accommodate these inconsistent behaviors and values.

College youth today seem to have assimilated the liberal values long emphasized in college courses and in the entire society. The college generations of the 1950s were often criticized for being apathetic and divinely self-satisfied, and for aspiring only to mar-

---

[7] P. Goodman, "Thoughts on Berkeley." In C. G. Katope and P. G. Zolbrod (Eds.), *Beyond Berkeley* (Cleveland: World, 1966), p. 78.

23

riage, a split level house in the suburbs, and a comfortable but not excessive income. Today, however, the most vocal students are espousing an interesting blend of the highest Christian and democratic values. Young people are concerned about the civil rights of Negroes. Those who participated in the McCarthy campaign evidenced faith in American democracy and an awareness of practical politics. Although frequently rejecting formal religion in an orthodox sense, many are nonetheless deeply religious. A recognition of man's need for others is one of the basic thrusts of the Christian faith. And youth also believe that those who do not reach out to help others lose their humanity. Although their tactics are frequently questionable, the young are concerned about war and are seeking other options. Those who enter the Peace Corps or VISTA speak eloquently through their act of the possibility of other alternatives.

Then, too, college youth today do seem, if not brighter, at least much more knowledgeable than were previous generations. Television, the paperback book revolution, and the drift downward into secondary schools of curricula previously considered college level have provided youth rich intellectual experiences from which, professors testify, they seem to have profited. And their knowledge has led them to seriously consider the many ethical dilemmas of the age. Knowing more of sex than previous generations did, they can openly discuss its role in such fundamentals as identity, relatedness, and security. Understanding science, they recognize that it is not a sacred cow, and they seek other, intuitive ways of examining questions of war, poverty, and violence. Being psychologically quite sophisticated, they search for appropriate instruments to enhance communication and a genuine coming together of people.

And this generation of college students has been reared in company with and has adjusted to powerful new ideas and instruments. Television, a completely different mode of communication, has brought youth into instant contact with the best and the worst of human life. Awareness that the genetic code will be deciphered and that life will be created artificially has forced the young to search for a new conception of the meaning of human existence, without the support of dogmatic moral postulates. Middle

24

class youth have experienced nothing but relative affluence but have been unable to cope with it successfully, for they have been trained in an ethics, sociology, psychology, and economics of poverty. And although they seldom discuss it, college youth have lived their entire lives aware of the possibility of atomic warfare and have had to adjust to the awful ambiguity of the future of human life.

College youth also reveal some highly undesirable and quite dangerous traits and tendencies. Partly because of psychological sophistication, they are too frequently self-excusing, preferring to place blame for personal imperfections on childhood experiences, parental failures, and the tensions of contemporary society. Possibly as an outgrowth of parental permissiveness, affluence, and the communications and transportation revolutions, youth currently reveal even more impatience than they normally have. In part this impatience leads to the undisciplined ways in which the young approach the solution of problems. They feel that their moral indignation is enough to unravel the issues of an unpopular war in southeast Asia. They want open hearings before a multitude as a way of deciding the disposition of a complex research enterprise. They generalize on the basis of limited experience at one college as to what is wrong with academic governance and how things could be corrected. And they tend not to view contemporary problems in the light of history.

Militant students especially, but others as well, tend also to reject the democratic processes or the processes of bureaucracy so essential for the functioning of a complex society. A small group of SDS students insist that their vision of reality and their ideas of morality prevail, even though they are contrary to the visions and ideas of the majority. They reject reasoned discourse and ordered debate in favor of violent confrontation. They view compromise, the essence of the democratic process, as a tool of a malignant establishment. They ignore established means of protest— political action, peaceful assembly, and persuasion—as they rush to sit in, destroy property, or vilify those in authority.

And there is in youth a dangerous romantic strain. As mentioned before, youth seems to believe in participatory democracy, the simple life, the virtue of the folk tradition, and the supremacy of feeling over cognition. Thus, they trust feelings of outrage or frustration and use them to justify even criminal assault, for which they believe there should be no reprisals. The young SDS members at Columbia who beat with a club a professor who stood in their way are of the same sort as the German thugs of the 1930s who beat and humiliated Jewish shopkeepers. The romantics want participatory democracy in place of what they see as an impersonal, manipulative, organized political process. True democracy to them means direct democracy, where the people's will is expressed by the people themselves rather than by their representatives. The founding fathers however clearly understood that a large nation required techniques of governance different from those of a small city-state, in which direct democracy by an elite did seem to work for at least one generation. This romantic faith in the people has led from Danton to Napoleon, and from Russian populism to Stalin. Unless curbed in America it could lead, as so many have predicted, to a fascist state.

After diagnosis must come prescription. How shall we deal with troubled youth? It seems axiomatic that a society which fears its children is indeed sick, yet the nation is drifting in that direction. Fear breeds punitiveness and vindictiveness, which only deepen the rift between the generations. Perhaps a first step should be a general resolve on the part of those responsible for the society not to become punitive regarding youthful behavior, no matter how frustrating and pathological some of it may seem. This resolve includes avoiding specific legislation to cope with campus unrest or campus violence. Legislation to penalize a category of persons invariably causes more trouble than it cures. Vindictive misuse of legislated sanctions should also be avoided. Draft reclassification is not an appropriate remedy for campus protest. Furthermore, legislators, board members, and benefactors should restrain from interfering with the administration of institutions, which must after all be able to deal with campus problems delicately but with requisite authority. In extremity a large society must protect itself by intervening in whatever institution presents the threat. But campus violence has not reached that point, and the experiences of Brandeis and Chicago suggest that the modern college or university does have the techniques to restore order and to dispense justice when it is free to do so.

More creatively, those responsible must realize that troubled youth, regardless of persuasion—radical, black, alienated, or beat—do have seriously unmet needs and legitimate grievances. Although the complaints of the young include much nonsense and quite foolish rhetoric, they also contain much truth. Youth does feel insecure in the large, impersonal institutions created to serve them. Young people do feel rejected when their teachers spend their time on research, consulting, and personal work rather than with students. College students generally feel cheated when they find that the courses they take are not of much value or significance. And they do feel resentful when they realize their need for help in making critical developmental decisions but find their colleges quite unconcerned. Thus youth should be heard and their valid needs should be provided for, tasks which require listening with a third ear. Such attention is now possible; a large body of information indicates what college students are like and what their needs seem to be.

But how should colleges deal with radical demands pressed in illegal and very frequently violent ways? How should they deal with the take-over of buildings, arson, confrontation, and irrational demands? The first imperative is to develop on campus a legitimate judicial system with codified processes and specified sanctions so that when offenses are committed, justice will prevail. An institution makes itself vulnerable if it attempts to deal with highly litigious student radicals in the older, less formal ways of administering punishment as a parent would. In the past discipline was viewed as an educational instrument which could be modified according to individual developmental needs. But times have changed. Now an answer to student complaints about the bureaucracy must include more bureaucracy. The campus judicial process must involve full student participation and institutional commitment to abide by decisions reached. Too frequently militant students have been given a legitimate cause because an institution did not follow due process or placed a student in double jeopardy or violated some other constitutional right.

Equally important is the need to force students in classes and in academic debate to abide by the same standards of scholarship and argument which the faculty member expects of himself and his peers. The faculty tolerates too much fuzzy thinking, speaking, and writing on the part of the young, partly one suspects because of some deep faculty guilt over abuses of student rights and neglect of their needs. Gradually, if students are forced to realize in classes that rhetoric alone is not enough, a rational climate may return to the campus. This approach, of course, is gradual and does not attend to the immediate crises; but it does approach an underlying cause.

Colleges should also have policies for dealing with student demands for major and rapid changes in institutional policy, such as immediate admission of an entire category of applicants, abolition of ROTC, shift in land utilization policy, or cancellation of defense-related research. Students should question such matters; but institutions have often been forced into precipitous debate and decision because of student demands for an open hearing. The institutional stand should be that such matters will be considered in due time and by proper agencies and that meanwhile there will be no negotiations over them. In spring 1969 Stanford, Brandeis, Chicago, and Cornell all allowed themselves to be faced with confrontations because they assigned legitimacy to extreme student demands. Then, faculty groups strengthened legitimacy by debating the issues raised. At Stanford, for example, student militants staged a sit-in at an engineering building to protest classified and defense research. The president, board, and faculty, in an effort to handle the problem within the university and to clear the building by peaceful means, debated and voted on the issues raised. A more appropriate stand might have been to refuse to discuss the issues during a time of crisis and confrontation. This stand, of course, would have forced a showdown and raised the possibility of using off-campus police. In retrospect, especially since police ultimately had to be used, it might have been better to do so at once, with safeguards against possible real or alleged brutality. Once a stand has been taken, the university should move quickly through established procedures to trials for and sanctions against students who have violated specific laws or regulations.

Presidents have been reluctant to follow this advice, partly out of fear of alienating faculty. But perhaps too much power has been allowed to drift into the hands of faculty, power which is inappropriate and which a deliberative body cannot wield. Power over such things as finances, internal security, and maintaining the university should be restored to the central administration. Faculty councils, senates, and the like properly should advise on or set policy but should at the same time mandate the executive to act.

The administration should also declare to students that many matters which affect their lives are ones over which they have no direct control or even direct voice. To name but a few: investment policy, the granting of tenure or the appointing of administrators, research, professional programs, and governance. All of this is not to suggest that students have no voice or that their attitudes and beliefs are unimportant or that an institution should in all cases take a hard line. Students should be allowed to determine their private lives; they should be heard on all issues as long as they speak within the confines of rational discourse or legal protest. Institutions must understand the complex situations the young face and allow considerable latitude, and they must tolerate awkwardness in discourse and protest. But reasonable tranquility will return to the campuses when a sense of community is recreated, a community in which the various interests can interact with mutual respect and through rational processes.

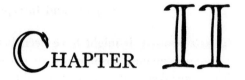

CHAPTER II

# Curricular Response

Colleges and universities cannot, of course, correct all of the ills of society or respond to all of the needs of youth. However, through the curriculum, that most expensive part of the collegiate enterprise, some of the development needs of youth can be met. By doing so, colleges at least might reduce student arrogance and make it less dangerous.

If student dissent were taken seriously and if the objects over which confrontations have developed were judged as what was bothering students, there would be no need to change the curriculum or styles of teaching. Except for those confrontations over black studies and black power, major campus upsets have not been about the central purposes of universities. Columbia students objected to a gymnasium, the Institute for Defense Analysis, and a prohibition of demonstrations in university buildings. At Duke the demands were for official statements of mourning for Martin Luther King, Jr., and pay increases for nonprofessional staff. Stanford students wanted an end to defense-based research. And at Berkeley the worst travail was over the university's fencing a plot of ground used informally by street people as a recreation area.

Twenty-two congressmen, in search of various reasons for troubled campuses, discovered that students were bothered but not about academic matters. Students felt they could not communicate with administration because institutions had become too large. They believed faculty spent too much time on research and counseling and that universities were hypocritical if they attempted to remain neutral on controversial issues. They were convinced that institutions overreacted to student disturbance and were too prone to use police power. They saw all these issues in the context of the broad ethical and social problems which bothered them—the military-industrial complex, hunger and poverty in an age of affluence, imperialism, the war in Viet Nam, the draft, and a vague feeling of remoteness from places of power. Students mentioned relevance but not what they thought was irrelevance.

Student writing and discussion bring the same message. Thoughtful militants are distressed about national priorities, control of the universities, lack of progress in protecting civil rights, and paternalism. The radical left see the university as a sick society in microcosm and want to destroy it. Meanwhile the large majority want visiting rights in the residence halls, better food, fewer regulations, new facilities, and the one general curricular concern, an end to graduation requirements. On some campuses students have prepared scratch sheets with caustic descriptions of courses and professors. And, when asked, students note that some professors are not particularly enlightening and that some courses seem a waste of time. But it takes searching to find such critical comments. Stu-

dents generally do not discuss, criticize, or, one suspects, even think
about what can be presumed to be the central work of the university
—teaching and the curriculum.

Colleges and universities, however, would be mistaken to
assume from this evidence that all is right with the curriculum.
Listening carefully to what students criticize and say they want and
attending to the form in which they express themselves reveal
serious flaws in the collegiate curriculum or at least somewhere in
the educational system. The intellectual style of much student protest is weak. As mentioned before, students are young and are still
learning; hence they can be excused some awkwardness. However,
at some point, education should have helped the young to understand that wishing for a simple, pastoral life does not make large
cities go away; that a historically derived rule of law is safer, for all
of its failings, than is the rule of men; that a simple sentence with
subject and predicate is clearer than one with "you know" inserted
after every tenth word; and that there are no simple causes of or
simple solutions to complex human problems.

More importantly, testimony of college students frequently
covertly reveals profound developmental needs which should be
but are not being met by the curriculum. Students are searching
for ways of understanding and eventually using emotions and im-
pulses. They want to be free and open to new experience, for they
sense that to be valid life must be embraced by the complete
organism. But the curriculum serves a narrowing, restricting function which students quickly discover is of little help for their own
development. When college freshmen encounter the orthodox curriculum of rhetoric, foreign language, mathematics, inorganic chemistry, and a survey of Western civilization, they turn away quickly
to the movies, rock music, athletic activities, and small group social
activities.

During late adolescence and early adulthood human beings
in American culture also need to reflect about themselves, about who
they are, and about their emerging self-identities. They require
some isolation in order to assimilate and synthesize the physiological
changes of adolescence, the changed role relationships with adults,

and the personal freedom which approaching adulthood offers. They require time to try to wring meaning from the new social or intellectual experiences available to them. But they discover and finally complain about the frantic pace which a full-time schedule of college courses imposes. They must work at five or six unrelated courses, jump from a history lecture to a German recitation to an hour divided into forty minutes of dressing and undressing and twenty minutes of physical education, and back to a chemistry lab. Students would probably tolerate such frenzy if they could be persuaded that there was a personal pay-off for them in it. But since they generally are not, they seek a countercadence to the fibrillating tempo of official collegiate life. They study one or two subjects and rely on glibness or pulchritude to pass the others. They attend classes at their convenience rather than according to the imposed schedule. And they seek intellectual growth in the leisurely hours of talk with friends rather than in professor-dominated classrooms. The point is illustrated by a brilliant Stanford student: "Undoubtedly I will not use nine-tenths of the course information gotten here at the university. . . . There's a difference between one's intellectual and one's academic life. In the past few years, I feel I've been taking courses that have little impact on what I do and that are not fruitful intellectually."[1]

In addition, although contemporary college youth appear to have rejected formal or orthodox religion, they nonetheless seem to be asking theological questions and searching for religious meaning. The quest for identity, commitment, and relevance (translated as meaning) which so preoccupies the conversation and writing of college students is a religious quest. The searches for a new sexual morality, for a reconciliation of man's moral inconsistencies, and for an ideal brotherhood of all men are at root theological concerns. And when courses in religion and theology respond in only archaic terms, when attempts in literature to deal with theological issues are obscured by textual criticism and concentration on writers

[1] Quoted in J. Katz and Associates, *No Time for Youth: Growth and Restraint in College Students* (San Francisco: Jossey-Bass, 1968), p. 242.

33

rather than their works, and when philosophy concerns itself exclusively with logic, leaving ethical questions unanswered, students turn to other sources. An appealing model for explaining contemporary student behavior presents students as searching for salvation. "They want to be saved—saved from the responsibility of perpetuating the world they see around them, saved from the dreary acceptance of life which they observe about them, and saved from the living death of the adult who rejects his own experience in deference to some authority with power over him."[2] The author of the model sees college students embarking on an extremely serious search for salvation within the tradition of wholeness of self, fulfillment, and social health. From such a vantage point much student activity can be viewed as theological and liturgical. Some seek salvation through the use of drugs presumed to open new dimensions of self-understanding. Others search in sensitivity training for an explanation of the insensitivity of society. Not finding salvation in the traditional religions of the West, still others have sought self-understanding and self-acceptance through Eastern religions and philosophies. Even student activism can be similarly interpreted. Much of it has positive and reforming goals for removing barriers or impediments to salvation. Andrew Greeley argues this same point when he suggests that the psychedelic represents in part a resurgence of man's need for the sacred in a secularized society. He points out that psychedelic drugs, rock music, beat communities, and the art of dissociation are all "ecstatic, primordial, contemplative, ceremonial, ritualistic, and sexual . . . all predicative of almost any religious liturgy that the human race has observed . . . a judgment for . . . past liturgical failure."[3]

Another related need is for esthetic experiences to which students can respond deeply; they intuit that the arts are properly means of emotional growth and when experienced directly contribute to self-awareness. They find, however, that the arts as taught

[2] D. L. Rogan, *Campus Apocalypse* (New York: Seabury, 1969), p. 9.

[3] A. M. Greeley, "The Psychedelic and the Sacred." In G. K. Smith (Ed.), *Agony and Promise* (San Francisco: Jossey-Bass, 1969), p. 209.

in college are historical episodes, objects chiefly of rational analysis, or exhibitions of an esoteric culture to be experienced only after extensive academic apprenticeship. The multisectioned course in art taught by means of daily lectures given in a darkened room with displays of slides is much too illustrative to be amusing. Student response is once again to search outside the curriculum for what they need. In rock and jazz, in homemade fabrics, in crafts, and in multimedia sensoriums, some students are finding esthetic experiences which reflect them and their age. The fact that thousands would journey to up-state New York and suffer physical discomfort to participate in a three-day rock concert, while only a few attend orthodox concerts, is bleak but eloquent testimony of curricular failure.

Another student need as yet unmet by the curriculum is for courses to be related to what students anticipate when they leave school. The future pediatrician or internist wants knowledge which will help him directly yet is forced into spending hours on gross anatomy. The student who wants to become a social worker or teacher and senses that behavioral sciences should assist in preparing for that role is told that sociology and psychology have little carry-over to the real world and should be studied as abstract intellectual exercises. In the past, students did not severely criticize courses in the sciences because they believed there was some relationship between the drudgery of their course work and what they ultimately would be doing. But in the social sciences and in the humanities and increasingly in the natural sciences students have become skeptical of and resistant to course routines which they see as largely unrelated to life. And as more and more students are drawn to the social sciences and humanities as a possible source of help for themselves and their society, widespread disillusionment appears. Not finding courses linked to reality, students have gone underground and created their own curricula. Professional students select from what is offered only those elements which they feel they need and demonstrate competence in the rest through various versions of gamesmanship. Other students compartmentalize their activities into largely irrelevant tasks necessary to obtain a grade and tasks to further their own education. These students run some risk of jeopardizing either their grade or their interests.[4]

There are many other needs to which the curriculum has not been responsive or has been responsive in limited and ineffective ways. There is a need for guidance to help students make academic and vocational choices. Students do need considerable help in developing social presence or intelligence. Students, especially in large institutions, need help in understanding and coping with bureaucratic and institutional life. They also need assistance in understanding their changing relationships with the major institutions of society. Evidence of all these needs is found in the language and acts of student dissent. But perhaps enough examples have been presented to suggest a need for curricular response.

Colleges and universities have begun to make curricular changes, partly in response to what they believe to be student needs and demands but as frequently in response to other forces and factors. Whether these reforms succeed depends in part on the primary motivation for initiating change. Those made for economic reasons or to satisfy faculty desires are largely irrelevant to the educational needs of college students or are antithetical to them. And they may even fail to achieve the purposes for which they were attempted.

The first of these curricular changes is the decline of general education as a distinct movement. General education was born at Columbia in 1918, was given form at the University of Chicago in the 1930s, was spread through the efforts of several of the great Midwestern universities in the 1940s, and was granted respectability through the publication of the Harvard Report in 1947. It consisted of prescribed interdisciplinary courses with behavioral objectives linked to man's nonvocational life. Although the number of required courses has not changed appreciably since 1957, their character has changed and will do so rapidly in the future. General

---

[4] The contrast between what students do for grades and what they do for their real education is well described by Howard S. Becker and others, *Making the Grade* (New York: Wiley, 1968).

education is being replaced by the distribution requirements popular in the 1920s and 1930s, which ask that students take a certain number of courses in each of the major divisions of knowledge. Ostensibly this shift provides flexibility for students, but actually it was brought about by a faculty unwilling to teach nondepartmental and staff courses. The academic climate was such during the 1960s that young Ph.D.s would not accept positions in which they had to teach staff courses, for they saw their future related to the department and departmental offerings. The reform of general education is not likely to improve the curriculum for students because the distribution system does not force faculties to create courses for the nonmajor. And even if the regression proceeds, as it has in a few places, to the free elective system, it still will not bring improvement.

A second category of reform consists of changes in academic calendars. Pittsburgh began the movement when it created the trimester to make the best use of scarce physical facilities. That effort was followed quickly by other attempts to gain year-round operation. Schools on the semester system changed to a four-quarter plan, and schools on the quarter system either tried the trimester or emphasized that the four quarters already ensured year-round operation. Then came the flurry of other temporal modifications. Some tried the three-three (three courses in each of three terms), the four-one-four (the one being a month of interim studies), the four-four-one, a three-semester academic year starting in early September so the semester ended before Christmas, and even a revised single-course plan (one course taught in seven weeks). These plans are spawned for a number of reasons: they are easier than curricular revision and make a faculty feel it is accomplishing something; they combat low faculty morale over the lame duck session after Christmas in the traditional semester; or they attract attention to an institution having something new. Perhaps the most cynical attempt was that of a major university which divided each quarter in half so that professors taught the first five weeks and students did independent study the second part, thus allowing faculty more time for their own work. Only with such a bribe could senior professors be persuaded to teach lower division courses.

37

Third, there are those reforms, not curricular but of technique, under the rubric of uses of media. These methods include use of open- and closed-circuit television, computer-based or -assisted instruction, language laboratories, tapes, recordings, multimedia classrooms, and programed learning. Once again economics motivated experimentation. Was it possible, through technology, to bring about savings in the instructional budget by presenting a professor to larger numbers of students, by shortening the time required for students to master a subject, or by making students responsible for more of their own education than they were previously, thus ultimately increasing the student-faculty ratio? By and large this goal has not been attained, and the use of media has not become central in higher education. There are, to be sure, thousands of experiments, and a number of institutions have developed large-scale programs for limited purposes. But the bulk of the college curriculum continues as though the electronic revolution had never happened.

A fourth major category of reform consists of different ways of grouping students and teachers. This change more than some of the other reforms has been stimulated for educational reasons. Examples of new groupings include team teaching at Chicago Teachers College, the house plan at Stephens, the experimental college at Hofstra, block scheduling at Florida State, the cluster colleges at Michigan State and the University of the Pacific, and the separately housed colleges of six hundred to one thousand students at the University of California, Santa Cruz. This last grouping was designed to capture the spirit of the older, small residential colleges in the context of a larger institution which provides needed economies of scale. Reports indicate some success with these changes. Students like the small groupings; and when students get to know one another well by being in a series of the same classes, they develop more rapidly than they do with other arrangements. If the serious problems of cost and faculty satisfactions can be solved, some form of regrouping may prove a fertile approach to reform. However, in the enormous state colleges and universities, where other ways of organizing are already built into the physical plant, the possibility of affecting large proportions of students still seems remote.

A central effort to change the curriculum in response to student needs is the attempt to create informal, issue-oriented courses and courses of differing time lengths. These changes originated in student creation of free university courses; and each set of recommendations following a campus upset includes provision for offering new courses and getting them approved through the administrative apparatus. Such programs as the experimental courses at San Francisco State, the freshman seminars at Stanford, and the new Freshman Year Program at Antioch have been well received. But difficulties abound. Quality control is an issue—that is, how to ensure professional competence in teaching a wide-ranging problems-centered course, or, if teams of faculty are used, how to afford it. Logistics also are involved—how to accumulate library holdings and make them available for constantly changing course titles. At Stephens College, for example, a junior year seminar, required of all students, changes its focus each year, and the library has not been able to keep up. But above all is the same problem which plagued the general education interdisciplinary courses—how to prevent informal courses from being superficial and conveying a false sense of sophistication to students who take them. Courses in personal adjustment and functional mathematics failed, and these new courses may fail also.

Another promising reform consists of providing off-campus experiences for students. These opportunities enable them, in theory at least, to test academic ideas in real life. When well organized and funded, these efforts have produced frequently dramatic results. Cooperative work-study at Antioch and Northeastern is essential to the impact those schools have on students; and at Northeastern, a university of 26,000, the cooperative work-study program allows it to be competitive with lower tuition public institutions. The overseas campuses of Stanford University are significant elements in a Stanford undergraduate education. Several questions arise however. If every institution attempts overseas programs, are there enough places to put students? Even now, parts of Europe which once welcomed students are much less open and receptive. The ghettos obviously cannot absorb too many more transients. And even in an expanding economy difficulties would arise in accepting cooperative study students from freshman classes of over two million. Cost is another factor. Smaller institutions already facing serious financial crises find the administration necessary for a full off-campus program too expensive. And if junior colleges should become the main route by which students receive their lower division education, can meaningful off-campus experience be fitted into a two-year program?

This analysis indicates the current impasse. Through implication, campus turmoil and student unrest have revealed student needs to be affective, esthetic, and moral or theological, coupled with the needs for a leisurely pace and for course content clearly related to the students' conception of the world. At the same time, students' language, perspective, conceptualization, and reality-testing should be sharpened to avoid some of the revealed pathologies. Curricular reform, although sometimes promising, has experienced or will experience logistical problems or financial difficulties if provided for large numbers of American undergraduates, especially in the larger institutions—and increasingly these will be the academic homes of most undergraduate students. The fundamental question remains: Can there be an effective curricular response to campus turmoil? Some progress might be made by thinking of the curriculum along several dimensions.

As the first of these dimensions, at least four different sets of educational experiences should be considered. The first set should provide a common universe of discourse—a common body of allusion, illustration, and principle—which is necessary for communication and for sharing the same culture. At one level this common set of experiences is provided by television, and partly by other mass media. However, other common experiences at a more sophisticated and richer level are desirable. The general education component of the curriculum should provide this common set of experiences and nothing more. A course should be listed under general education requirements only if it is useful to all people living in the last

40

quarter of the twentieth century. Because the entire curriculum cannot be composed of general education courses, the choices should be made in the light of conflicting and contrasting values.

A second component of the curriculum could be called liberal studies; it should consist of courses which students take to broaden their experience and to sample or explore different fields, frequently on a very liberal basis. Liberal studies, for example, would be courses in the arts or social sciences taken by a specialist in one of the hard sciences or mathematics. They probably should consume approximately a fourth of a student's curricular time.

Then there are those courses essential for a major, or concentration, and another group of courses which could be considered as contextual. For a history major, courses in political science, economics, or even psychology would be considered contextual, while for a physics major, courses in mathematics and chemistry would be contextual. Although no hard and fast percentages can be posited, as a rough guide (engineers, nurses, and teachers pose particular and peculiar problems), general or common education should constitute a fourth, liberal studies a fourth, contextual studies a fourth, and a major a fourth of the student's undergraduate years. To increase the weight of the major beyond a fourth begins to distort the purpose of the undergraduate curriculum and to approximate the mission of advanced professional or graduate education.

For the general education part of this curriculum, a traditional program could consist of a course in the humanities, stressing the Western tradition and probing into selected artistic, architectural, philosophical, and literary expressions of various ages; a course in social science, interrelating materials from sociology, anthropology, psychology, economics, and political science; a course in natural science, either interrelating materials from both the physical sciences and the biological sciences or stressing one or the other; and a course in communications, developing writing and speaking skills. Such a curriculum at least samples the broad domain of human knowledge and is defensible in the light of orthodox traditions of the liberal arts and sciences. However, it may be vul-

41

nerable to the charge that it still does not consider the concerns which commonly perplex not only college students but the entire adult population of the nation.

Another program of general education would be spread throughout the four undergraduate years. A course on ethics and theology in the contemporary idiom would raise and discuss questions like these: What is the proper stance for a conscientious objector? What are the theological implications of heart transplants? What are the ethics and the theological presuppositions of the growing feeling of the need for law and order? Another course might involve law, economics, and the organization and structural conditions of a postindustrial society rapidly becoming urbanized. This course would seek to help students understand themselves in relation to an increasingly complex society. A course in literature would present students with a wide range of literary materials, some in contemporary idioms, to evoke esthetic and emotional responses, and would avoid extensive analysis. A one-semester course in writing and an elective chosen from a limited pool of courses created to meet general education needs would complete a student's program.

This total curriculum should be structured so that students are almost forced to elect experiences different from those in which they specialize. These experiences are here labeled as liberal or broadening studies. Probably most students benefit from some concentrated work in a limited area, if only for the sake of seeing just how complex a single field is. The major, or concentration, is supportable; but that concentration is much more meaningful if it is done in an appropriate context.

In addition to these different sets of educational experiences, a second curricular element is strongly suggested by the kinds of demands and criticisms undergraduate students have advanced. They sense that they need various experiences if they are going to develop in a comprehensive way. The several described below do not constitute a necessarily exhaustive list.

Every student should have the opportunity to engage in independent study in which he sets his own goals, proceeds at his own rate, decides when he has finished, and feels free to use or not use professorial resources. This independent work should not be confused with a scheduled tutorial arrangement, where the volition rests with the professor. Rather, it should be the opportunity for students to succeed or fail on their own.

Every student should learn in large and impersonal situations. Adult learning goes on through mass media or in large group lectures or the like; and college students should be able to learn in this way without feeling threatened or particularly lonely. Thus at least one large lecture course might be part of the experience of every student, with no discussion groups, laboratory groups, or further assistance provided.

But students also need to learn to function in small groups and do need the encouragement which a small group can provide. Thus the curriculum should be structured so that in some way every student has a sustained experience in a small group, and the time should be long enough so that the group can take on many of the characteristics of a primary group.

Every student should have a relationship with an adult professional person which is sustained over a long enough period of time so that the adult can serve as an appropriate role model, parent surrogate, and friend—someone with whom the student can test his emerging notions of reality. This relationship is probably the most important single experience students require.

Every student should have a sustained off-campus experience. Whether this be cooperative work-study, an overseas experience, or the opportunity simply to study on one's own in a distant city is less important than that the student be encouraged to look beyond the campus walls.

Every student should have the opportunity to know intimately a culture or subculture different from his own. This knowledge may come from studying in a foreign university, from doing cadet teaching in a subculture substantially different from the student's own, or from serving as a participant-observer in a distinctly different subculture.

Every student should be required to make a sustained effort

43

over a prolonged period of time on some task. Some courses, possibly quite a few, should extend over a full year or more, with assessment left until the end. The traits to be developed here are not unlike those generated by work on a doctoral thesis.

Every student should have opportunities to engage in a number of brief informal activities which have the same curricular value as longer, more sustained efforts. Students should be encouraged to experiment and explore but should not be expected to make major time commitments to such activities. A number of explorations might consume no more than a week or two.

Every student should enjoy, unpenalized, opportunities to engage in play for his personal satisfaction.

Every student should have opportunities to gain deeper understanding of his own emotions and those of others. Sensitivity training, group therapy, individual counseling, or similar activities can lead to this understanding.

Every student should have a chance to learn by using some of the new media. He should learn something with the aid of a computer and with a programed course using audio and visual aids, direct observation, and reading. The new media are so important that college graduates may be considered illiterate if they have not learned to use them.

Every student should have an esthetically creative experience regardless of the level of his performance. This requirement suggests some form of studio work done just for the satisfaction of creating something with physical materials or sound.

These experiences should all result in certain student competencies which education is obliged to provide. The following skills constitute a third element in the curriculum. They are desired and needed by students, demanded by the society into which they will move, and of legitimate concern to college teachers. To read, write, speak, and listen with some sophistication in subjects of concern to people living in the last half of the twentieth century. To recognize personal problems and issues and to be able to resolve them with the use of the best available information and assistance. To know and to be able to use a library and other bibliographic aids—not only printed matter, but other media. To cooperate intimately with others in solving complex problems. To distinguish between cognition and affection and to be able to use both rationality and feeling. To be able to relate in both evaluative and nonevaluative ways to other people, and to understand the appropriateness of each response. To be able to enjoy one's own activities without threat or guilt if those activities are unusual and not commonly valued by others. To be able to identify gaps in one's experience or learning and to find ways to fill them. To understand computers and other ways of arriving at quantitative knowledge and to recognize both the capabilities and limitations of quantification. To know and to be able to express one's own values and to defend them and modify them when occasion requires.

The fourth and final element of a model curriculum is probably dearer to the academicians' hearts than the three previously elaborated. This element has two components. The first involves the major divisions of human knowledge which come into existence and subdivide through research and inquiry. Obviously, the subjects listed in a curriculum are determined by the mission of an institution, by the training and experience of its faculty members, and by the needs of the clientele served. However, all students should be exposed to some knowledge of the Western European tradition, American civilization, at least one non-Western civilization, the broad domain of science, and some technology, mathematics, and quantification. And they should do some interdisciplinary work which suggests how various subjects illumine each other.

The second component consists of the several ways of knowing, ranging from the starkest sort of empiricism at one extreme to intuition and revealed truth at the other. Since all humans must make use of these different ways of perceiving reality, the college curriculum should at least sensitize students to the attributes, capabilities, and limitations of each. With the demands college students currently are making, overemphasizing the descriptive, the phenomenological, and the intuitive is probably wise. Such emphasis would come through courses in philosophy, the arts, and theology. Thus, concepts of empiricism, experimentation, and statistical

45

manipulation could be contained in courses in the natural sciences or behavioral sciences. Mathematics could be taught empirically, descriptively, or even esthetically.

This four-part model is eclectic and is not intended for exact duplication at any institution. Rather, it suggests a way of thinking about curricula in times of enormous social change. Its purpose is to declare that the contemporary college student needs and can have a contemporary curriculum.

CHAPTER III

---

*Students in*

*Governance*

---

I f the curriculum were made germane
and if professors would attend to the needs of students, there would
be less student demand for a major substantive role in academic
governance. Running colleges and universities is a difficult, complex,
time-consuming task requiring highly developed technical and pro-

47

fessional skills. Students do not have the time, experience, or talents for these tasks. Yet, until they sense that colleges and universities are seriously trying to meet their educational needs, they will quite arrogantly and presumptuously demand a voice. The solution to this dilemma is obvious.

Primary considerations in any discussion of student participation in governance are what students have been demanding and whether some degree of involvement in academic governance could meet those needs. These needs were expressed, analyzed, criticized, and subjected to probably too much publicity during the last half of the sixties. But they remain and must be responded to. As we have seen, first and foremost, college students want personal freedom and control over their private lives. Next, students demand the free exercise of their civil and political liberties, including the right to plan on campus political action to be taken elsewhere and the right to hear speakers regardless of persuasion. Then, uneasy and concerned about the great moral dilemmas of the society, they want their colleges and universities to help them do something about those uncertainties and to become part of the quest for a moral society. Especially in the largest institutions, but even in the quite small, they wish for less impersonality. They are irked by bureaucratic procedures and being treated as numbers; they want to count as individuals. They demand some voice in deciding institutional goals and priorities, although the vast majority remain relatively unconcerned about this matter. And equally, and for the most part inarticulately, students ask for improved education, a relevant (that is, contemporary) curriculum, and even improved teaching. A small minority of radical students claim more—participatory democracy (meaning frequently a rule of a new elite—themselves), control of the university, use of the university as a major instrument of social change and revolution, and destruction of the university as a first step in the destruction of the entire society. Out of these desires, yearnings, and aspirations comes the notion that institutions will become responsive only if students can set rules, review budgets, sit on committees, and have a say in selection of faculty.

## Students in Governance

If student demands were all that were involved, a system of accommodation could be quickly suggested. But there are other factors. A number of significant changes in higher education make the problem of academic governance much more complex than ever before. As a result of student protest, student control over their private lives has increased in even highly protective institutions; even the courts are beginning to recognize that the concept of *in loco parentis* is dead and that equality of the sexes is a reality. Whether they will like the honor after the euphoria of revolutionary times has faded, students do sit on faculty committees, are consulted about presidential candidates, and on occasion are elected to boards of trustees. And the successful student use of force, aided for obscure reasons by some faculty and given an intellectual rationale by some apologists for youth, has forced presidents to yield some power and authority if not directly to students at least to the faculty. This delegation of power may be one of the most profound changes and one which students may one day come to regret. In many institutions presidents have yielded so much that they no longer have the power essential to govern. With the loss of that power students lost a powerful ally against their real but unrecognized enemy, the professionalized, entrenched, and syndicalist faculty. Finally, as a result of student protest have come a political and public disenchantment with higher education and a climate of opinion which will make needed resources difficult to obtain. As educational affluence ends, students will find many of their demands resisted as institutions discover they can no longer afford the luxury of uninformed student dictation of policy. In 1969, for example, students at Stanford, with considerable faculty support, demanded that a defense research controversy be resolved by bringing Stanford Research Institute directly into the institution. This resolution was economically unsound, and in 1970, in spite of warnings of student protest, Stanford sold the institute with no restrictions placed on the kind of research it could do.

Other changes have also taken place. The lay board of trustees, an essential innovation in American higher education, has lost the power to govern since control over information essential to

49

decision-making has been assumed by the complex bureaucracies which even quite small institutions have created. Boards do, of course, appoint presidents and assign legitimacy to decisions, but the substance of decision-making lies in the recommendations various offices prepare. Then, too, in the public sector, statewide coordination or control systems have assumed powers over budgets, programs, and processes which can be touched only with difficulty by presidents, bureaucracies, or boards of individual institutions. These agencies are equally impervious to student influence and react negatively when attempts are made to bring such influence to bear. Relatedly, systems of institutions and institutions themselves have finally embraced the concept of long range planning based on complex data. To be ratified decisions must be consistent with the goals and benefits established by long range plans. This requirement creates inflexibility in responding to the spontaneous demands of students for changes which one student generation can see accomplished.

Another kind of inflexibility has come with the successful academic revolution, which gave faculties enormous power over themselves. Faculties feel that they must protect the fruits of this revolution in this generally regressive period. This hegemony of faculties was made possible because of the high demand for professional services during the 1950s and 1960s. It allowed faculty members to be somewhat tolerant of demands of students for some privileges, as long as they did not ask too much. But market conditions have changed, and professors can be expected to be less charitable toward those who threaten the status quo. One liberal professor who encouraged various student protests but then saw cuts in his own research empire remarked, "I have come to hate student activists for having destroyed my style of life." Then, there is the steady growth of unionism among college faculties. Although the ultimate significance of the union movement is unclear, a union contract, oriented toward the economic well-being of professors, probably will not accommodate student demands for professorial services above and beyond the call of duty. Reduction of impersonality will not be served by a contract calling for nine hours of teaching, three office hours per week, a graduated salary schedule based on tenure, and ensured tenure appointment under threat of grievance proceedings.

Perhaps the greatest change of all, and one implied by these other changes, is the loss of high public regard for higher education. Three periods can be identified since World War II. The first, from 1947 to about 1957–1958, was a period of courtship, when colleges and universities, having become significant through successful wartime research performance and accommodation of veterans, promised the society much in return for support. The period from 1957 to approximately 1967 was a honeymoon during which the entranced society judged education as the chief instrument of national policy and offered support in the largest outpouring of favorable legislation, both state and national, in the history of the country. Then came disillusion. Higher education did not produce the good life. But it did seem to produce a generation of revolutionaries, which was not what adults had had in mind. And so from 1967 onward higher education has experienced curtailment of support, increased political control, and a climate of opinion generally unfavorable to intellectuals. Reactionary times are not favorable to democratic or egalitarian ideals.

Besides these changes which have taken place, another element in the equation is how well students have performed when given some responsibility for academic governance. Unfortunately little systematic evidence is available. However, on faculty committees, unless the students are espousing a particular radical cause, they have been silent, speaking rarely, and then in tones of the establishment. During fall 1969 in a half dozen institutions in which students sat as members of committees, they adopted the self-imposed role of junior members responsible for the menial tasks of keeping minutes and ordering the coffee. Students were most productive when concerned with regulation of student life, campus judicial activities, and cultural events. And they were least productive and too frequently most destructive when dealing with critical decisions of institutional life. On such grave matters as tuition increases, restriction of graduate enrollment, changes in tenure policy, genuine curricular reform, and deficit financing students did not seem to make critical decisions. They made interesting and insightful observations, but for the most part these matters were decided elsewhere, with the wise precaution of counseling with or informing student groups. Unfortunately there have been some destructive performances, as when student leaders tried to make public the information in stolen confidential personnel records or leaked to the press the names of candidates on the list of presidential search committees.

The very nature of academic governance is also involved in deciding what role students should play. John Corson[1] points out that colleges and universities, in common with other organizations, exist to accomplish something, require resources, must have processes to enable people to work together, and move either forward or backward. But colleges and universities serve a multiplicity of purposes and are more dispersed as enterprises than are other organizations, with responsibility for decisions more widely diffused. "The central objective of a college or university is the translation of the talents and capacities of its faculty into significant educational results."[2] If students are to have a role in the governance of these academic institutions, their contribution must be unmistakably clear and explicit. And their role must have relative strength but of a different quality from that of the faculty or administration. Otherwise, although students may be involved, that involvement will not be central to the life of the institution. In the American system of higher education faculties have generally been conservative with respect to educational and institutional matters. This conservatism regarding curricula, innovation, status, and the like ensures the stability of an institution, which otherwise could be shaken to pieces by too rapid development encouraged by the administration, the dynamic agent for change. The administration seeks innovation, change, progress, growth, and new missions, and the faculty generally thinks otherwise. Much of academic governance is a search

---

[1] J. J. Corson, *Governance of Colleges and Universities* (New York: McGraw-Hill, 1960), pp. 8–10.
[2] *Ibid.*, p. 113.

for ways to bring these two forces into creative tension. Institutions in which the faculty is too strong tend to atrophy, while institutions in which the administration is too strong tend to overexpand and move toward rank and uncontrolled growth. Student demands imply the creation of a third force, but the nature of such an element is unclear. Students could, consistent with the balance of power theory, side first with administration and then with faculty against whichever seemed to be growing stronger, but such an attempt would put students in the peculiar position of acting constantly against their own interests. Joining with faculty against administration would strengthen faculty syndicalism, which emphasizes faculty needs and desires, while opposing faculty would strengthen the power of the bureaucracy, against which much of the student protest has been directed. Governance is ultimately the resolution of conflicts brought about by the differing needs of individuals and groups dependent on the institution. For the stability of the institution someone or some element must have the final power to resolve such conflicts. In the American system of collegiate education this power belongs to the board of trustees and is exercised, although increasingly imperfectly, over such matters as the allocation of financial resources, the setting of institutional goals, and the relationship of the institution to other legitimate institutions in society —the military, business, government, and labor. To become a truly third force students should have the information, the legitimacy, and the resources to precipitate conflict over such matters. Students would, for example, need a power equal to that of the administration over the budget or of the faculty over the curriculum. They do, of course, have the negative power to go elsewhere and, during the 1960s, the negative power to bring an institution to a halt. But use of these powers is against their own interests, as students at San Francisco State have discovered. Since neither faculty nor administration can perform their essential roles without the power they now have or have at least in theory, they will most likely not yield these to students; presidents cannot yield power over administrative appointments without jeopardizing their effectiveness, and faculties cannot surrender their power to select their own members. Thus, the very nature of governance suggests that if students have a role, it must be a minor and subordinate one.

The complex of factors, the nature of student demands, the changes which have taken place in higher education, the evidence of student performance in governance, and the reality that legitimate power is essential to government imply that students do not have a central role in academic governance given the presently recognized central objective of colleges and universities. However, there is also the implication that since collegiate institutions do exist to serve students, as consumers they should have a voice to indicate, and with some force, whether their needs are being well or poorly met.

First among the factors to be considered is the fact that the governance of even a small college or university is a complex undertaking requiring enormous data, little of which can be comprehended by students, who presumably have an education to acquire. Consider if you will what is required to decide whether to expand the University of Hawaii medical school from two to four years. First, nationally there is a need for more doctors, but should Hawaii, with only one million population, be asked to provide them? Hawaii needs to develop, but along which lines: sugar, pineapple, tourism, or what? Since it has a two year school, is it better to ship students to the mainland, where medical schools are already overflowing, or to expand advanced capacity? And if this is done, what is the greatest cost-benefit advantage—a four year medical school or an expanded East-West Center (a graduate research center affiliated with the University of Hawaii)? These are complex questions. The spokesmen for youth say the young clearly cannot answer them, but they can answer questions of broad policy. This is fine in rhetoric, but broad policy to be meaningful must answer detailed questions, which, in turn, require detailed knowledge. And detailed knowledge requires detailed study. But the young, who already complain of the frantic pace of academic life, cannot be expected to undertake it. Yet the young who would govern say, "We can set priorities then let the administrators work out the details." Consider another example. A college, to remain financially viable, must maintain an adequate cash flow. To do so an amount is budgeted each year for building replacement. This amount then provides the security to underwrite periodic loans from a bank. The man who developed this scheme spent twenty years to make it work. Can a student, with four years to spend on an education at his parents' expense, hope to comprehend even this relatively simple problem and still acquire the skills which have become so important in a postindustrialized society? Several other examples. To develop a scheme to improve admissions requires the full time of five professionals for three years. Can a young Negro, conditioned as he is by racial injustice, have the sheer technical expertise needed to solve such a problem? Or, an institution is running a deficit of over two million dollars a year. A change in investment policy can rectify at least part of this. What changes will the youth whose allowance of fifty dollars a month is coming from his schoolteacher father make?

There are broader questions. Students desiring to govern say, "But if we have faith in people, such details will be unimportant. Participatory democracy will allow the wisdom of the race to prevail." However, this notion runs counter to another fact of life. Because of the condition of modern university life, constitutionalism is the wave of the future. To ensure reasonable working conditions for people in a large scale enterprise, there must be constitutions, bylaws, handbooks, and quite specific codes of behavior with specific penalties for offenses. This fact of life is contrary to the belief of students that if people simply get together and talk and feel, all will come out all right. No matter how much the young may complain, decisions for large scale institutions must be made through bureaucratic means, and these decisions will frequently irk those who want instant solutions to complex problems. This problem is well illustrated by some of the young who have experienced complex educational processes and who want to change it all. They assume that once they have a degree they can become dean or president and change the world. Their goal in itself is revealing. They want to become the new elite so as to remake an imperfect world in their own image. With constitutionalism, which protects rights of persons, the processes of change are slowed to a

rate which human beings can cope with. The four or six or eight
years of a bachelor's program are not long enough to see major
changes take place. If the rights of all are to be preserved, instant
solution must be subjugated to the slower process of constitutionalism, which says, "Before appeal to the agency for resolving
ultimate conflict, recourse must be had to the administration and
lower courts."

A third fact having considerable implication for student involvement in academic governance is the still remarkable diversity
in kinds of institutions. Global pleas for participation overlook the
differences between San Jose State and a large public junior college,
in which most students come to the campus for courses and then
leave at once. In many public junior colleges the evening enrollment is double the day enrollment and is composed of people taking
one or two courses after work. To suppose that such a group
either could participate actively in governance or could be happy
being represented by a minority of students who attend the day
session strains credulity. The few institutions having long and successful experiences with students in a central role are relatively
small liberal arts colleges in which a sense of community developed
in response to real and pragmatic needs, as was true at Antioch
when it faced the financial crisis during the depression of the 1930s.
Since most students attend large complex institutions with many
commuting students, the problem of significant representation in the
central administration seems insoluble. If there is student participation, it most likely would come from a minority of resident students,
a system which would be as contrary to democratic ideology as
would presidential rule alone.

Size is also related to another development antithetical to
significant student participation in governance. That development
is the increase in privatism and the significance of quite small
primary groups in the lives of students attending large and, for the
most part, impersonal institutions. Increasingly students cope with
the neutrality of daily campus work—class attendance, library
work, and laboratory exercises—by being members of small intimate
groups seeking to preserve their own interests. Although these

groups are maintained by some form of tacit democratic effort, they are not structurally organized to be a political basis for campuswide representation. For example, at Stanford, students who attend an overseas campus at the same time form such primary groups regardless of where they live. Or, graduate students living in the same married student housing units form such groups regardless of their fields of concentration. This development does not mean that some system of representation could not be created—living units, classes, registration status, and the like. But it does suggest that such an organization would be artificial and without political significance.

However, another factor which also must be considered does require, in spite of difficulty, that students have a voice in at least some parts of the conduct of institutional life. That factor is the generally older student body on campus caused by such developments as students' returning to college after various interruptions—war, work, marriage—and the steady growth of graduate enrollment. Large numbers of students are physically and legally adults but have not yet achieved full adult status, which comes with economic self-sufficiency. Such individuals wish to have and need considerable voice in decisions regarding their lives and conditions. The questions are in which parts of institutional life should they have a voice and how ensured should their participation be in light of these other facts and forces.

A structure of campus governance could be devised which would be based upon principles which maximize the chances of achieving the goal of governance—that is, conversion of faculty skills and knowledge into educational results—and which at the same time safeguard individual rights, whether they be those of the students, the faculty, or the administration. First, a system of checks and balances is necessary to ensure that the tendencies of one branch or constituency encounter opposing tendencies of others in such a way that a creative rather than a destructive tension is produced. Thus, the conservatism of faculties should encounter the dynamism of central administration so that the institution neither dies for lack of change nor changes too rapidly. No action of one branch should be exempt from review by the other.

Second, such a structure requires definite constitutionalism expressed in written documents—faculty constitutions, bylaws, grants of power to students—which specify the responsibilities, processes, and procedures of each of the constituencies and the various steps which must be taken in making decisions affecting individuals. In the past institutions could be governed with few rules partly because of the homogeneous quality of most campuses, which ensured a shared set of common values, and partly because institutions were not overly complex. There could be general agreement as to what conduct as a gentleman and a scholar meant. But conditions have changed, and the significant common culture must be expressed in writing, with the implication that all matters not covered are of no institutional concern.

The third principle is essential, although it was seriously challenged in the 1960s. This is the principle of legitimacy—some agency must be generally recognized as supreme. The United States assigns legitimacy by declaring the Constitution to be the supreme law of the land. Colleges and universities have been assigned legitimacy by states, which have the power to create corporations with indefinite tenure and to lodge responsibility for those corporations in boards of trustees. As the legitimate agencies, boards of trustees have the right to make whatever decisions they wish for the institution limited only by the stated purposes of the charter and the appropriate laws of the state. Many of these powers can be delegated but not finally, for some agency must make final decisions and resolve conflict within the institution. Were there no boards of trustees some other agency would have to be created to wield its powers, gaining legitimacy either through force, general acceptance, or documentation. Without a legitimate agency to resolve conflict, any institution would destroy itself through the efforts of different constituencies to gain their own ends. This power to resolve conflicts should rarely be used if institutional checks and balances and guarantees of procedural rights operate. But without this power, especially in times of high emotion, the conflicting desires of faculty, students, and administration over the employment of controversial professors, for example, when pushed ultimately, would result in the state's exercising its sovereign power and resolving the conflict by politics—an event not to be desired.

The fourth principle is that information, authority, and responsibility cannot be separated. No one should be assigned responsibility without having direct access to the information essential to the task. For this reason purely faculty committees cannot work because they do not have direct access to the information in administrative offices. No one should be given authority without definite responsibility which ultimately leads to the legitimate source of power. Thus, no faculty curriculum committee should be given authority over course offerings without responsibility for ensuring that its decisions do not jeopardize the institution. Thus, a president could return a curricular proposal to a committee on the ground that acceptance would jeopardize the financial security of the institution. To apply this principle to student participation in governance, consider such an issue as university investment policy, which is one means of achieving the end of governance. Students would first need information (and this is highly complex); then they would need to be responsible and accountable so that exercise of authority did not weaken the institution. Only then could they participate significantly in such a decision.

The next principle is implied by several others. No person or office should have the right to make decisions about people without the explicit provision for review. No dean or president could decide alone to expel a student, terminate prematurely a faculty contract, or reclassify a clerical worker. If decisions are made consistent with established and written policy, review would rarely be necessary. But the right of and procedures for review should always be ensured.

In the light of these principles, the nature and purposes of colleges and universities, and the conditions of large size and complexity, the rights, duties, and responsibilities of various elements can be suggested. In public higher education especially, various coordinating agencies have evolved to ensure statewide planning, wise utilization of resources, and achievement of state educational policy. These agencies are buffers between institutions and the political arm of the state. In general they should not be given ultimate power because they are not sufficiently close to the information upon which responsible decisions must be based. Rather, they should have a role like that of the House of Lords in the English system. That is, they can debate and make public broad policy and can postpone but not stop decisions from being implemented. They should be composed of distinguished laymen but should not include representatives of institutions, who tend to be self-serving.

Boards of trustees should clearly have the power to appoint chief executives, assign legitimacy to critical decisions, and resolve ultimate conflict. But in general they should not attempt to make decisions, for they cannot have the essential information, which is lodged in the administrative bureaucracy. As a general rule board action should be taken to ratify proposals made by a responsible administration with, of course, the right to change the administration proposals if it sees fit. Boards can and should discuss issues and help keep an institution informed of social needs as they see them. And they should help interpret the institution to the larger society. But boards generally should not attempt such administrative tasks as revision of tenure policy, faculty appointments, or regulation of student conduct.

Presidents and central administration should generally have power over budget allocation and control, administrative appointments down to and including those of department heads, certain veto powers, and the power to represent the institution publicly. In the exercise of these powers administration should be bound by established procedures, policies, and checks. Thus a president could not announce a new concentration in Italian studies without the prior approval of the faculty, for curriculum is the province of the faculty. However, a president could veto a recommendation for a tenured appointment on the ground that the institution could not sustain a financial investment of that magnitude.

The faculty should have almost irrevocable power over its membership, the curriculum, and the conditions of student entrance to and exit from the institution. These powers are essential if the purposes of governance are to be achieved. Thus the faculty could refuse to approve a faculty appointment no matter how strongly urged by central administration and could, within the limits of relevant law, decide which students could and could not enter and what conditions students must meet in order to graduate. Faculty exercise of such powers would be checked by the opposite powers of administration, for the most part through persuasion and discussion but finally through an absolute check.

As for the students, they should have power over their private lives subject only to the limitations imposed generally on people of that age and limitations made explicit in college catalogs, ratified by boards of trustees, and applied universally to all students. Thus, if an institution wishes to serve only those of a particular religion or to ensure that all students live in college residence halls, it may do so. However, it may not make exceptions or go contrary to existing civil law. Students also should have the right of due process and should have access to courts if their civil rights are curtailed. They also should have procedural rights approximating due process for matters peculiar to institution life. In addition they should have the right to be consulted on the effectiveness of the education they receive. Students should participate in governance but not as any warrantable right. Rather, participation could be suggested as an additional educational experience which the faculty judges will help individual development.

CHAPTER IV

# Faculty Militance

$\mathcal{J}$ust as frustrated students contribute to unrest on the campus, so do professors and for similar reasons. The academic revolution has given professors exalted ideas of their own importance. Yet the expansion of higher education has not provided them enough time to become socialized to the roles of academic man. And the very size and impersonality of complex systems of higher education have left professors feeling powerless while desiring great power. They respond with petulance, arrogance, and anger.

# Faculty Militance

Because of the kind of people they are and the nature of their work, college professors have always been a mystery to those outside the university. They frequently seemed preoccupied with precious or trivial distinctions, demanded legal protection for their jobs not accorded other vocations, and assumed the right to criticize even the most hallowed beliefs of the society. Their visible workday seemed comparatively short, and they rejected the idea that what they did might be supervised. They considered themselves to be the university, not employees of it. Such traits and behavior have generally been tolerated because there is a generally understandable rationale for them. The search for truth requires refined instruments of analysis which to the outsider may appear trivial but which, when applied, can frequently expose universal insights. And because truth can threaten orthodoxy, some protection is necessary if one is expected to inquire with objectivity. Although a lecture consumes only an hour, preparation for it can frequently take a lifetime. And in theory a university is nothing more than a guild of scholars each seeking and speaking truth according to his own discipline.

But during the 1960s some professors, for seemingly inexplicable reasons, began to manifest behavior and to make demands which puzzled and troubled not only outsiders but administrators and board members. It seemed almost as though a new breed of professor had evolved. Once disdainful of trade unionism, professors, especially in junior and state colleges, began to experiment with collective bargaining, applying economic sanctions, and finally striking and refusing to cross picket lines. San Francisco State and St. John's University are only the tip of the iceberg of faculty trade unionism. For over three centuries American professors had been content to allow deans and presidents to secure funds, build buildings, set salaries, and handle the details of governing with the stipulation only that the faculty be allowed to pursue its own work without interruption. Suddenly professors began to demand not only a share in governance through academic senates but veto power over every act of administration; they theorized that presidents and deans were but chore boys for the faculty. One can speculate that some of the uncertainties of college presidents over student protest resulted from unsureness as to how organized faculties would react.

In the realms of politics and public policy professors of the past had more frequently than not been content to remain isolated and remote or to criticize in historical or theoretical terms. They believed that the university, to be free from political interference, should itself refrain from political activity. But suddenly professors began to speak out on the most controversial political questions, to engage in direct political action, and even to suggest that the universities they served should, as institutions, oppose the war in Viet Nam, oppose the draft, and refuse to conduct defense related research. Some went even further, joining with militant and protesting students to force changes in institutional or public policy through strikes, sit-ins, and confrontation. Some, particularly younger faculty, also began to adopt styles of dress and grooming similar to those of students—long hair, beards and sandals, and psychedelic dress. In student protests it is frequently difficult to distinquish students from faculty.

Through such actions, as well as through the power generated by favorable market conditions, faculties have made strong and unusual demands and interesting decisions. They have pressed consistently for lighter teaching loads and more time for research, even when a majority of faculty members were not interested in or qualified for major research efforts. In the emotional climate generated by the war in Viet Nam, faculties have eliminated ROTC and urged administrations to reorganize investment policy so as not to support defense related industries—judgments which likely would have been different had they been made in less turbulent times. And a few faculty members have almost created their own systems of ethics, as when a history faculty refused to assign any grades rather than withhold grades from a few students who had been suspended for protest activity. Then, too, there is a growing uneasiness on the part of activist faculty that the system will proscribe them for their political opinions, coupled with a willingness to generate student protest to support their beliefs. One upset at the University of Chicago stemmed from just this situation.

# Faculty Militance

The facts of growing faculty unrest are relatively easy to document. The American Association of University Professors (AAUP) has gradually moved from its pristine conception of itself as a professional organization to a stance which allows collective bargaining and strikes under sufficient provocation. Stimulated by the abortive strikes at St. John's University, Catholic University of America, and Chicago City Junior College and by the aggressive recruiting efforts of the American Federation of Teachers (AFT), the AAUP shifted to support of the principle that faculty should not be denied the opportunity to strike because of either societal needs or the long run interests of the university.[1]

From the early 1960s on an interest emerged and sometimes was even legislatively mandated in the creation of faculty senates as a way for faculties to participate in institutional planning and governance. Some of these bodies recognized that administrators had contributions to make to senate deliberations, but a fair number limited senatorial membership and courtesy to classroom teachers. And a few senates wished to be responsible to boards of trustees, thus putting themselves in an adversary relationship to presidents of institutions. Reflective of the new climate the American Association for Higher Education (AAHE) supported a study of governance as a means for providing shared responsibility. Historically the association had not taken a position on such matters but did so tacitly after the report was published.[2]

For long, teachers and especially college professors rejected membership in trade unions as being inconsistent with their image as professionals. However, in the early 1960s first in New York City and then elsewhere the AFT as an affiliate of the AFL-CIO won rights to represent teachers and to engage in collective bargaining, and called and won strikes even when prohibited by law. The union began to attract college faculties and increased its membership in colleges, especially in those state institutions located in large

[1] "Faculty Participation in Strikes." *AAUP Bulletin,* 1968, *54,* 155–159.
[2] *Faculty Participation in Academic Governance* (Washington, D.C.: American Association for Higher Education, 1967).

northern cities. Although the AFT has not gained exclusive collective bargaining rights in any collegiate system, it has forced votes and has put other organizations on the defensive.

These successes forced the National Education Association (NEA), previously an exponent of professionalism for a unified profession, to elevate the stature of its largest unit, the Classroom Teachers Association, to develop first a system of economic sanctions and then to recognize strikes as legitimate, to compete outrightly for members with the union, and in the sphere of higher education to develop a militant Junior College Faculty Association dedicated to a strong adversary relationship with administrators. And various faculty groups have been instrumental in the passage in over ten states of legislation requiring either collective bargaining or a definite decision by faculty not to engage in collective bargaining.

Two questions arise. Why, when college professors are better paid, more respected, and more sought after than ever before, has there been an increase in trade unionism, direct political action, demands for faculty hegemony, and willingness to join with militant students in sometimes violent pursuit of common goals? And, what is the appropriate institutional and social response to such behavior? Answers to these questions can be superficial, dealing with the most apparent causes and immediate responses, or they can involve fundamental elements. In spite of the temptation to search for quick resolutions, it seems wiser and more healthy to probe for root causes which can then lead to lasting changes.

First there is an economic reason. College teachers for generations were exploited financially. Indeed the low salaries paid teachers before 1957 subsidized the education of college students. After 1957 the rapidly rising returns from teaching made even greater financial rewards seem possible. Higher expectations were also sharpened by the fact that other professions and occupations were improving their economic positions at an even faster rate, and in effect they established a model for the professors to emulate. Much of the effort to unionize has been with the purpose of improving the economic position of professors, and the same motive in part underlies faculty interest in governance. Perhaps the first demand a newly created faculty senate or faculty association makes is to examine the budget. They suspect that the budget will reveal large sums used for administrative or other "inappropriate" purposes which could be diverted to the service of professors.

Second among relevant factors are historical patterns and structural changes within higher education. The most obvious of these patterns is the preeminent role assigned to boards of trustees and to presidents. The American college evolved when few well educated faculty members were available. Instruction was carried on by tutors who were not presumed to have the ability to be responsible for an institution. Responsibility was assumed by board members, who, because distances were great, assigned power to the president to raise funds and buildings, recruit students, register them, and handle the important parts of instruction himself. This simple structure worked, at least reasonably well, until the expansion of higher education at the end of World War II. Since then institutions have struggled to find new ways of reaching decisions and conducting business, and as experiments failed, faculty members have put forward the notion that they could not do much worse. One reason faculty members have sensed the need for greater involvement is that on too many occasions during the postwar period presidents and their administrative associates have just not been responsive to changed conditions. Colleges have doubled or tripled in size, have quadrupled budgets, and have taken on more building in a decade than they had in two centuries, but the administrative structure has remained the same. An alert faculty eager to determine policy came into existence at Columbia only after the historical system of governance revealed itself unable to cope with student unrest. Careful clinical study of thirty institutions experiencing curricular problems revealed that the central problem was a failure of the administrative structure to keep pace with institutional growth. As the central administrator, the president was gone too much and left no power at home adequate to cope with day-to-day work. Sensing a power vacuum and conscious of their increased power, faculty groups have attempted to move in.

In addition, as higher education became large, complex, and expensive, suprainstitutional boards and commissions were created in most of the states, and power was transferred from the campus to statewide bureaucracies. Thus, faculty members no longer knew who made decisions or how, and they felt they had lost their opportunity to intervene. Since faculty members, as professionals, believe they have the right to control themselves and since older ways were no longer open, they searched for new techniques and instruments for regaining influence over their affairs. Unions, statewide systems of senates, and direct political action at the legislative level seemed appropriate. And when these devices failed to affect the bureaucracy, some faculty were willing to turn to more radical efforts. In one sense the joint faculty and militant student outbursts at San Francisco State, Berkeley, and the City University of New York, although sparked by specific incidents, resulted from frustrated attempts to influence decisions made by the impersonal system.

Other structural changes can also be advanced as relevant to faculty militance and efforts to extend faculty power. The increase in the number of administrative subspecialties (housing, admissions, financial aid, institutional research, innovation, and the like) has resulted in an elite, and the perquisites which attend their offices attract the envy and the attacks of the democratic mass, the faculty. The rise of student power threatens whatever hegemony faculties hold and hence fosters faculty demands, under the banner of legitimacy (students are only transients), for greater voice in governance. The expansion of the higher educational bureaucracy (AAUP, NEA, AAHE) has created professional workers whose futures depend on increased membership, budgets, and influence. Thus this bureaucracy seeks to rationalize greater faculty voice in policy-making and administration. After all the struggle between the NEA and the AFT is over membership, for through membership flows bureaucratic influence. But none of these reasons sufficiently explains the sudden explosion of faculty demands and the fact that demands are different according to the institution. At a deeper level causes must be found in the feelings, desires, and frustrations of individual human beings. Once again several hypotheses can be suggested.

Feelings of powerlessness on the part of professors are aggravated by an underlying feeling of insecurity, which seems endemic in academic man. Sociologists describe marginal men as people who have left one group or culture and who are striving to enter another but do not make it. Marginal people are characterized by feelings of anxiety, frustration, and quite often rage. In a sense many academic men are marginal. Some, with lower class backgrounds, use intelligence and education to move into the higher classes of society. As college professors, they have many of the attributes of the higher classes but still do not make important social, economic, or political decisions. College professors, even when in demand as consultants to business and government, are still not of the power elite. Other professors develop marginal status and feelings in different ways. The former high school teacher, now in a junior college, wants to be considered a real college professor but lacks the full credentials, the publication record, and even the freedom to create courses patterned on his own interests. Professors who teach in teachers or state colleges which are converted to comprehensive universities also become marginal. The catalog tells them they are university professors and that research and graduate education are important, but they possess neither the skills nor the interest to engage in such activities. The result is these feelings of insecurity and anxiety which professors seek to relieve through striking out at the system or organizing to defeat it. The most fertile fields for unionization are junior colleges and state colleges in transition, which have a high proportion of faculty who are desperately trying to leave the high school or teachers college category but without success.

A somewhat related phenomenon involves rather deeply imbedded feelings of guilt and attendant efforts to alleviate them. College professors, especially in the large research oriented institutions, realize that as they seek to achieve professionally through research, publication, and consulting, students, both undergraduate and graduate, are slighted. Rewards come faster from nonteaching activities or seem to. And since professors are honorable men, they feel uneasy and guilty about not giving as much attention to their students as they should. Since the demands of their profession make relief through giving more time to students impossible, other devices are used. When younger faculty members make common cause with protesting students and even adopt their dress and mannerisms, they are saying, "See, we really do love you so much that we try to act as you do." And more established professors try to alleviate guilt by protesting that they would like to teach undergraduate students but the system just does not allow it. Thus, the system, the institution, or the administrators become the scapegoats and fitting objects for criticism and rage. Faculty support for student demands to eliminate ROTC, to involve students in administration, to have instant redress of grievances rests at least in part on an attempt to make up for faculty neglect of students.

And fear plays a part. Underlying much faculty unrest is the recollection of the McCarthy era and a belief that only faculty hegemony can prevent a return to that proscriptive time. As state governments move toward a conservative fiscal and social stance, faculty militance increases, thus ensuring a downward spiral of act and counteract. A less altruistic fear may be for job security as hundreds of new institutions begin to produce thousands of new doctorates. The old guild spirit of limitation of membership is constantly present. It is reflected in debate about which junior college teachers should be allowed to join AAUP, about curtailing graduate enrollment in prestige universities, and about denying full acceptance to upstart state colleges which seek enlarged graduate enrollments. The guild spirit is translated into a desire for syndicalism and a longing look at how British faculties control themselves and the university. Then, too, there is the fear on the part of young scholars, trained to expect research grants, that such sources are drying up. Major professors lament that good universities have produced good research workers who now must look to teaching since there are no longer enough grants to go around. And graduates feel that if the war and draft could be ended, once again they could be supported in their work. So large do the draft and the war loom in conversations of graduate students and young faculty that one suspects ulterior as well as altruistic feelings. Others fear how the marketplace operates or may operate in the future. The eleven thousand dollar a year associate professor of history in an Ivy League school who sees his way blocked in that department but whose entire training makes him reject a state college in the Midwest is a prime candidate for participating in militant crusades against the system.

Of a radically different order is the fact that institutions have expanded so rapidly that older ways by which faculty members were inducted into academe have broken down. Before World War II a new faculty member remained as an instructor or assistant professor in the same institution for twelve or fifteen years, during which he learned of the various roles in a college or university and how properly to relate to them. He spent his entire career in one or two institutions and accepted the fact that change in a university comes slowly. Now, however, institutions grow so rapidly and have such an appetite for increased staff that young professors can anticipate constant mobility, for if one institution does not meet their demands, another will. Constantly changing positions and expecting and receiving instant gratification of desires do not allow for gradual enculturation. In a sense, unprofessorial behavior on the part of young faculty members results because rapidity of change has never allowed them to learn how to be college professors in the older meaning of that term. Young professors who refuse to meet classes if students are punished by legitimate judicial bodies for illegal acts and who strike against their institution for purely economic gains have just not assimilated the concept that professional service to students is the professors' highest obligation. They do not realize that the academic profession is in essence different from business and industry and that strikes for higher wages only imperil professional values—"the service ideal, the moral basis of professional claims, the commitment to shared and cooperative

71

decision making, the commitment to reason, and the pursuit of distinction."[3]

Before leaving this matter of root causes, and by no means have all been exposed, I stress that faculty militancy as well as student militancy reflects widespread unease about national and social priorities, inconsistencies between national ideals and national practice, and serious malfunctioning of a postindustrial society. Faculty members are concerned about the war in Viet Nam, the overemphasis on defense, the destruction of natural resources, and the plight of the underprivileged. And they, as all, feel frustrated when traditional or orthodox ways of solving social problems do not work. Out of such frustration comes a willingness to try new remedies, and some of these cures are distressing to all.

How should society, legislators, administrators, trustees, and colleagues respond to recent professorial behavior and its causes? No matter how vexing those responsible for financing and maintaining higher education find unionized faculties threatening strike, faculty efforts to emasculate administrative powers, public faculty demonstrations for unpopular causes, or even faculty participation in direct protest activities, punitive legislation or attempts to punish or to apply other sanctions are not appropriate. They can lead only to an increased polarization, which in both the short and the long run is unhealthy. Furthermore, many of the developments need to be accepted, for they are part of the change sweeping society. Greater faculty involvement in governance is a certainty and a healthy development. With the current social backlash against protesting students, there will be strong temptation to proscribe faculty and protest their behavior as faculty members ally themselves with students. But to yield to that allure would be a serious mistake. Tolerance of others in times of rapid change and heightened tensions is essential if new institutions and life styles are to be created; and they must be.

[3] S. H. Kadish, "The Strike and the Professional." In *Dimensions of Academic Freedom* (Urbana, Ill.: University of Illinois Press, 1969), pp. 51–59.

# Faculty Militance

Relatedly there should be no attempt to limit academic freedom, no matter how unpopular or controversial the subjects professors choose to explore. The American university has grown great in direct proportion to the academic freedom exercised by its professors, and this freedom must be preserved at all cost. It may be embarrassing to a president for a young professor to publish a letter advocating premarital sex or for a senior professor to be placed in jail for participating in a protest march against the war in Viet Nam, but this embarrassment should not be converted into punitiveness.

There are positive things to be done also. First is an elaboration of the concept of a corporate faculty, shared responsibility, or cooperative governance. This concept implies that boards of trustees, presidents, and other administrative officers are prepared to surrender some of the prerogatives which they historically have assumed and utilized. Junior college presidents must give up the pretension under which so many operate that they have the wisdom and insight to recruit and select strong faculty members in all fields. Liberal arts college presidents must deny that their standards of personal attire can be imposed on faculty members. Beards, after all, are not their business. State college presidents must realize that faculties can select committee members as wisely as did presidents in earlier times. And presidents in complex universities must allow others to have an important voice in the architectural style of new facilities. But the concept also implies that faculties cannot have the powers which central administration needs to maintain institutional vitality and viability. Chief among these, of course, is financial power. The president is responsible for the continuance of the institution and cannot yield control over the budget. Thus, the president must have a veto over such decisions as tenure appointments, for, among other reasons, a tenure appointment is a heavy financial obligation. The corporate faculty idea can be realized in a number of ways, not necessarily through a senate. A senate is merely a device to be used when the size of the faculty becomes so large that it no longer can conduct business. As long as there is a clear delineation of responsibility for faculty and administration

73

and as long as procedures are well established, recorded, and respected, any of several structures will work.

Second, but quite related, administrative officers must be prepared to act, but to act in noncoercive or nonvindictive ways and with full consultation with those affected by their decisions. Central administration can no longer afford the luxury of discouraging faculty from purchasing homes because to do so would make them feel too secure. It can no longer consult with only the board of trustees and treat the institution as a business corporation. It can no longer declare such matters as the religious stance of a college as not being open for negotiation. It can no longer make rulings after the fact on published professorial views about sexual behavior. In short, discretionary action will no longer be tolerated. To violate this injunction will be to invite faculty reprisals just as much as close scrutiny of the private lives of students invites student protest.

In the past university administration has been quite secretive about such matters as budgets and long range plans. This secretiveness has resulted in a climate of suspiciousness which probably made demands for power more intense than they would have been. Some matters must be kept secret for a time, but generally the facts about admissions, finances, building plans, and hopes for expansion could be shared with the full university community—faculty, students, and the several publics to which institutions respond. Here legislators have a specific responsibility to accept increased candor in good faith and not to penalize an institution for revealing in public that its enrollment projections were off. If administration would make information, both good and bad, generally available, tensions would gradually recede, as examples illustrate.

Because institutions are complex and will become even more complicated, there is need (as mentioned in the previous chapter) for more constitutions, bylaws, written rules of procedure, and the like. Many of the specific episodes which have jeopardized good faculty-administration relations, such as those which became cases for the AAUP, have happened because procedures and processes were not written in sufficient detail to guide action. In the past, institutions could and did function quite effectively with a minimum of documentation. However, in large organizations written policies and procedures are essential to facilitate smooth human relations. It is pertinent to recall that formal etiquette developed largely in the French court in the seventeenth century to make the close living at the court tolerable. Wise administration, therefore, should ensure that a constitution governs the division of power, that bylaws indicate how such critical matters as curricular decision or appointment and promotion are handled, and that all are conscious of what rights and prerogatives they have. This suggestion implies specific grants of power from boards of trustees to administration and faculties so that resultant organizations will have significance.

In part faulty faculty expectations have been created through faulty or nonexistent long range planning for an entire system. Thus without plans individual institutions may aspire to changing their character and may promise faculty graduate programs and research opportunities when the state will not support such developments. Or a faulty plan may designate that some institutions will become comprehensive universities, thus creating expectations for changes which are beyond the resources of the state. In either case faculty become disappointed and search for scapegoats—not a difficult task on most university campuses. In most cases of low faculty morale, probing reveals that exact expectations were not communicated to faculty members or that imprecise ones were or that expectations of faculty at the time of appointment had changed by the time decisions on promotion and tenure were to be made. In a former state college turned university in the 1960s half of the faculty were led to believe that teaching was important, only to find after transition that the rules had been changed and that research had become the route to advancement.

In another area, faculty members, like students, experience loneliness in large complicated institutions. When institutions were small and faculty cadres stable, newcomers were at once accepted by various small groups—residents in a college-owned apartment house, members of a small department, or residents in a college dominated neighborhood in the community. The situation now, however, is radically different in the large institutions located for the most part in urban areas. Faculty homes are scattered throughout the city. Departments are larger than they were a few decades earlier, and the persistent mobility ensures that no lasting primary groups or even friendship groups are formed. This loneliness contributes to frustration and anger, which are too frequently reflected in on-campus behavior. For both faculty and students significant small groups must be contrived. What is needed on a broad scale is a program with the force of a cluster college or an overseas campus. One can conceive of counterparts to presidents, deans, and directors who would have no administrative or norm-setting role but who would be available to help faculty members with personal or professional problems. Or, trained counselors might be made available, not just for students, but for faculty as well. Scholarship and teaching are often lonely quests and individuals in their loneliness need help in sustaining themselves. If somehow loneliness and insecurity were relieved, militancy might be relieved at the same time.

Then there is the device well illustrated in the *New Yorker* cartoon which pictured two executives talking, one of whom remarked, "I don't say it will work, but has anybody tried offering Walter Reuther a vice-presidency?" Administrators develop a global view of an institution and respond differently from the faculty member preoccupied with his discipline and department. Place a faculty member in an administrative or even quasiadministrative position and he begins to think in large terms. Very likely institutions, no matter how small, could arrange for every senior professor to have some broad administrative responsibilities to let him hear the drummer to which deans and presidents must listen. As a stark administrative principle appointing young turk professors as assistant deans for a year or so might alleviate considerable faculty tension.

At a different level some consideration should be given to channels of escalation. In highly centralized systems of governance small episodes of unrest at the base of the system quickly move to the apex, and in the process gain in severity. In the California state college system, for example, the events on a single campus can, within several days, become state political issues simply because of the centralized system with political figures located at the apex. Ideally the roads for escalation should be deliberately confused and confusing so that a tension-provoking incident may normally move in a circular route and end up back with those who started it. What is called for here is the administrative equivalent of the road net of Paris deliberately designed to slow down and disperse the mob. Channels there must be, and they must be recognized as such. But they should be well spaced with diversion points so that the route to confrontation is not inevitably followed.

These suggestions are all intended to improve underlying conditions. But in tense times some consideration must be given to the immediately disruptive or disturbing situations. Consider the situation of a young, somewhat unkempt sociology instructor, without a Ph.D., who nonetheless has been appointed for two more years, who has been outspokenly critical of the administration, his colleagues, and the entire legislative process. One day in connection with a disputed use of a college facility, he leads his sociology class of about forty to a sit-in in the questioned building for perhaps three or four hours with the intent of dramatizing their need for the space in preference to that of the physics department. There is no violence in connection with the episode, but the news media do cover the event, public indignation is aroused, and the legislature, in session, is urged to apply sanctions through cutting back appropriations. What is most urgently needed is time, so that decisions can be reached through due process; hence no precipitate action should be taken by anyone. Then, the institution, using legitimate machinery, should obtain all available facts. If they suggest that indeed there has been a violation of campus regulations, the matter should be placed before a campus judicial body with jurisdiction over faculty affairs. The administration has no choice but to serve as the plaintiff and to seek whatever penalty it judges appropriate. But the decision must be made by the legitimate judicial body, and the administration is bound to accept the outcome with the one exception of having the power to reduce a penalty. If the president is pressured by his board of trustees or the legislature into taking arbitrary action, this action simply sets the stage for the next confrontation, which, as practical men, both board members and legislature should want to avoid. If campuses throughout the country create legitimate machinery for resolving controversy and if it is used with all deliberate speed and with full understanding of the forces which determine aberrant conduct, the intensity of campus upsets will be considerably lessened. College students and militant faculty can properly be charged with impatience. But the proper response is not equal impatience but rather time, toleration, and temperateness.

# CHAPTER V

# *Fruits of*
# *Academic Revolution*

W hat makes faculty frustration and dissent so destructive is that it allows potentially lethal traits, always covertly present, to surface and become operative. Thus conservatism, attention to detail, pride in accomplishment, and willingness to use one's knowledge for public good are positive values until distorted and misused through feelings of anomie and powerlessness but with possession of actual and real power.

The successful academic revolution, which allowed higher education to become a major growth industry and faculties to gain virtual hegemony over their institutions, has produced impressive gains. The public supports higher education better than it has at any other time, faculty salaries have risen, and public regard has elevated the university to a pivotal position in American society. But this same revolution has tempted college faculties to indulge in a variety of vices, some traditional and some newly discovered, which could, unless restrained, reverse the outcomes of the revolution and render higher education in America redundant. Vice here implies a moral fault or blemish detrimental ultimately to health or usefulness.

Among traditional vices faculty conservatism is the most endemic and hurtful. College professors do not like educational change and will not undertake it unless forced by an external power (for example, students), bribed by financial inducements, or persuaded by powerful leaders. The great innovations in higher education were all generated outside the faculty and imposed over faculty opposition. The elective system, the general education movement, the reform of medical education, and the adoption of the model of German graduate education are reforms associated with Charles Eliot (president), Robert M. Hutchins (president), Abraham Flexner (foundation official), and Daniel Coit Gilman (president). Outmoded practices, however, are associated with the faculty: meaningless language requirements, awkward academic calendars, and archaic entrance requirements.

To this conservatism is added the equally bothersome, even if less hurtful, vice of pedantry, or preoccupation with unimportant detail. To the professor who spends years discovering a fact, that fact becomes all important, as do all other facts regardless of whether they contribute to student development. Pedantry accounts for a semester course in sociology devoted to the first few pages of Plato's *Republic,* taxonomic lectures in the biological sciences, or endless recounting of biographical data about authors rather than consideration of literary works themselves. Pedantry is no place more fully revealed than in the critiques professors make of each other's writing, well exemplified by the critic who rejected a manuscript submitted by a colleague for publication because "on page 2, line 2, the use of the word *behooves* is not justified by Webster."

Intellectual narcissism must also be listed as a vice. It permits professors to judge as a philistine anyone not sharing their esoteric knowledge. It is reflected by the professor who reads his mail during oral examinations but who expels students who sleep or yawn or knit in his classes. Its most virulent form is expressed in the syllogism "I am a specialist on Joyce; I am an educated man; anyone wishing to become educated should know almost as much [never as much] as I do about Joyce." This reasoning lies behind the inflated curricula from which students must select their courses and programs.

Although scholarship ideally stresses tentativeness and willingness to change opinions in the light of new evidence, much professional practice suggests distinct feelings of infallibility. Lectures from decade old notes imply a belief that nothing new can be added, and anger at student interpretations different from the professor's own indicates considerable conviction of correctness. Some forces reinforce these feelings of infallibility. The lecture platform does give a sense of power, and sycophantic students persuade the teacher that he does have most if not all the answers.

To these relatively innocuous vices the academic revolution has brought some which are potentially destructive. In the 1960s, with an undersupply of college teachers, faculty members first improved their financial conditions and then demanded and received greater voice than they had before in academic governance and control of institutional destinies. Presidents and boards of trustees, fearful they could not hold faculty who were denied power, accepted faculty associations, senates, and the claim that the faculty was indeed the essence of the university. Fearful of the prospect of an investigation by the AAUP, grown influential with its report on faculty salaries, presidents yielded to faculty demands for re-

vised tenure procedures until their appointive power had in some
cases almost eroded away. In some state institutions tenure almost
comes with appointment. Sensing complete victory, faculty then
contended that it was quite capable of governing an institution
without the detailed knowledge or experience which had accumu-
lated in the presidency or the finance office. Particularly when this
newly won power was directed toward financial matters did it take
on the characteristics of a serious vice. In one institution, reliant on
tuition for operating funds, the vice-president for finance had each
year budgeted $200,000 to $500,000 for capital expansion or replacement. From these funds the institution managed to provide
the needed facilities and to enter the decade of the seventies relatively free from debt. The faculty, feeling in control after having
produced a new senate and constitution, wanted to redirect those
funds to what it considered to be a much more important use, con-
tinuation of increases in faculty salaries at 5 per cent to 10 per
cent a year. The faculty was unaware that without an adequate
cash flow the credit of the institution with the banks would end
and with that an end to flexibility would come. When a major
university announced a policy of curtailment of expenditures rather
than face an increasing annual deficit, faculty groups wanted to use
the powers of the senate to force a less prudent policy, in spite of
available evidence that extramural funds for higher education were
declining.

A second destructive vice derives from several different
phenomena associated with the academic revolution and the World
War II era and is probably characteristic of a minority of faculty.
College students in the 1960s frequently came from highly permissive homes but still needed parent surrogates to help in achieving full adult roles and identities. Although these students rejected
the notion that the university should take the place of their
parents, they needed to relate rather intimately with an adult.
Some faculty members also had the psychological need for the self-
perpetuation which could be secured by having disciples. This need
had probably always been present but in earlier times was satisfied
through the protectiveness institutions and their officers assumed

over student lives. In the 1950s and 1960s, however, some professors came to view students almost as children who could do no wrong. Frequently in order to gain the love of these children surrogates, faculty would pander to the basest sentiments of a student mob. Thus professors with straight face contended that the American middle class college student, inheritor of the greatest material and intellectual largess the world has ever known, was as much victimized by his college as were the Jews in Nazi Germany or the Negroes in a Jim Crow South. These middle aged apologists for youth, such as Harold Taylor, Paul Goodman, John Summerskill, and Edgar Friedenberg, exemplified the vice of demanding less from the young than they would from themselves. This vice appeared in those faculty who reveled in the mob violence at Columbia, who urged amnesty at Harvard or Stanford, or who joined the student strike at San Francisco State in support of Negroes in pursuit of unobtainable and unjustifiable goals.

Then the academic revolution, by placing faculty members in demand by government, industry, the international community, and other institutions, stimulated the vice of pride. If someone is asked to advise on million dollar appropriations, on the conduct of foreign policy, or on new industrial products, that call must indicate personal superiority. And if one is superior then the chances are he is superior in most if not all things. Thus the biologist expects to be taken seriously when he espouses a political view; and he expects his demands for support to be granted over all other claims because he knows best what is good for society. Nowhere is this almost arrogant sense of personal worth seen more clearly than in prestigious universities, whose faculties judge it their right to have decreased or nonexistent teaching loads so they can get on with what is important, their own work. At such institutions faculty lunch conversations revealing who has been in Saigon, who is in Paris, and who has been called to the President's Task Force on Education are gamesmanship among the anointed, not serious intellectual conversations.

But in at least one domain faculties have gained absolute power, and it is as corrupting for them as such power is for political leaders. Through the power to evaluate students and to recommend them for jobs or advanced training faculty have enormous influence. Before World War II this influence was not of great significance because the middle class youth who attended college were not that concerned about the opinions of their professors. A gentleman's C could be obtained with little work and would still qualify one for Wall Street or medical or law school. But as the pressures of numbers allowed institutions to become selective, professorial certification became critical. A low grade or a mild letter of recommendation could deny a student a degree, a chance to enter medical school, or a position at a desired institution. Grades became the legal tender of the academic subculture and professors the bureau of engraving which regulated the flow of currency. Since education had become the principal point of entry into many vocations and since professors controlled entry, they found themselves in a position to determine the character of the next generation of leaders. And since they tended to favor their own sort it was likely that the next generation would resemble them—a not altogether happy thought. By 1969 some of this power over persons had been reduced through student demands for revised grading standards and less permanently damaging forms of appraisal. But the power is likely to be regained as colleges and universities produce more trained people than can be used effectively by the work force. Then the Ph.D. who gains the most desirable post will be the one most praised and rewarded by his professors, who once again can become arbiters of the national professorial life.

A vice difficult to describe but potent in its effect is the tendency, particularly among younger faculty trained in research oriented universities, to substitute methodological elegance for thought about reality. Statistics has replaced theology and philosophy, and a tight design for the study of insignificant phenomena is preferable to a looser but more searching exposition of serious questions. Unvalidated organizational theory substitutes for knowledge of a field, bibliographical critique is the chosen instrument for intellectual history rather than the clear analysis of trends, and the single star of reinforcement theory guides young scholars rather than trust in the multiple sorts of evidence which interpretation of human behavior warrants and requires. A corollary to this preoccupation with method is awkwardness with language—especially spoken language. Having learned to trust a borrowed theory, formula, or cryptic citation to esoteric but undigested literature rather than firsthand experience, these young scholars have not forced themselves nor do they force their students to deal verbally with complex and serious issues. Thus one young philosopher argues with his hands and assumes comprehension through the repeated injunction to his hearers of "you know." The danger lies in the fact that methodological elegance and verbal inarticulateness are inadequate to cope with either the needs of society or even the educational needs of students.

The last vice directly attributable to the academic revolution is the essence of the revolution itself—the tendency for faculty and institutions, as they succeed in currently accepted terms, to grow impervious to the explicit needs of society. Thus prestigious institutions, assuming a steady increase in research funds, cease preparing people to practice a profession and concentrate on finding support to allow the faculty to do what it wishes. Courses are designed with a view not to the educational development of students but simply to the intellectual interests of professors. Professors adopt a mandarin style which places professional development higher than the development of those who seek their services. And those in lesser institutions aspire to follow the same route. This desire stands behind the struggle of state colleges and even liberal arts colleges to offer graduate work, to conduct research, and to become centers of academic excellence—a course which amounts to faculty syndicalism enthroned.

These vices would not be too serious were it not for the fact that higher education has become significant in the life of the nation: people look to it for solutions to vexing problems, and it has become essential in a merit-based society. Furthermore this institution is expensive and will become more so (an increase in cost from 2 per cent to 3 per cent of the GNP in a seven year period). To what extent these vices jeopardize essential functions and how significantly they contribute to unnecessary increases in the cost of higher education are issues which must be explored.

To begin, faculty members do not have much significance in the lives of students. Performance on the Graduate Record Examination is related much more to the traits and abilities students brought with them to college than to what a given institution did for or to them, regardless of the prestige of the college or the quality of its faculty.[1] Students attach little importance to getting to know their professors or to getting recognition from them outside of gaining a desired grade.[2]

> Most students seem to be moderately satisfied with their colleges, though with no great sense of enthusiasm or excitement; perhaps inevitable processes of adaption lead to taking things for granted. Their attitudes toward faculty members are somewhat similar; students typically report little personal contact with them, and many students are often reasonably content to have it so.[3]

In addition, faculty continue to resist innovation and change, except when creating new programs to meet expanding vocational needs, even when the need for change can be reasonably demonstrated.[4] Warren Martin points out that a generally accepted norm of institutional excellence has developed and that as institutions approximate that norm, they are reluctant to change or even to tolerate suggestion of change. "A school's educational philosophy as well as any efforts at innovation and change are made to support the standard. The academic revolution of the last fifty years is now a revolution become counterrevolutionary, bent on crushing rivals and blocking further change. Deviation from the norm is not toler-

---

[1] A. W. Astin and R. J. Canos, *The Educational and Vocational Development of College Students* (Washington, D.C.: American Council on Education, 1969), p. 145.

[2] J. Katz and Associates, *No Time for Youth: Growth and Constraint in College Students* (San Francisco: Jossey-Bass, 1968), p. 26.

[3] K. A. Feldman and T. M. Newcomb, *The Impact of College on Students* (San Francisco: Jossey-Bass, 1969), pp. 257–258.

[4] JB Lon Hefferlin, *Dynamics of Academic Reform* (San Francisco: Jossey-Bass, 1969).

ated because it would be a challenge to the supremacy of this new behemoth."[5] Even B. Lamar Johnson, who usually can find positive evidence for both junior colleges and professors, finds innovations attempted on junior college campuses only when clearly defined faculty interests are served and when some powerful or respected figure serves as an agent of change.[6]

Another effect of faculty vices is demonstrated in the faculty response to the 1964 to 1969 student protests, which disrupted American college campuses, especially those campuses on which faculty had a high degree of professionalism and of personal prerogative. The faculty role in those episodes was not particularly creative or helpful. At Columbia a strong central administration encouraged faculty to perform almost as independent professionals, each attending to his own work and not required or expected to contribute to the central purpose or unity of the institution. Faculty thus led a pleasant detached life and had created no mechanism to cope with crises. Faculty detachment was part of the cause of student unrest and part of the failure to deal with revolt when it happened.[7] At Stanford in 1968 a majority of the faculty of humanities and sciences, which prides itself on being the highly departmentalized heart and soul of the university, voted in favor of amnesty for students who sat in at the Old Union. This vote brought a defeat for both administrative policy and the recommendations of a legitimate committee on reform of campus judicial affairs and quite directly paved the way for serious confrontation campus politics the following year.[8] At Duke, a faculty seeking professional excellence became segmental participants, absent from the campus a great deal and teaching what concerned them rather than what interested students. Their attitudes were part of the cause of student outbreaks.

[5] W. B. Martin, *Conformity: Standards and Change in Higher Education* (San Francisco: Jossey-Bass, 1969), p. 228.

[6] B. L. Johnson, *Islands of Innovation Expanding* (Beverly Hills, Calif.: Glencoe, 1969).

[7] *Crisis at Columbia* (New York: Random House, 1968), p. 34.

[8] J. McEvoy and A. Mutter, *Black Power and Student Rebellion* (Belmont, Calif.: Wadsworth, 1969), p. 161.

Then the faculty and an informal faculty senate undermined the power of the central administration to deal with emergencies and eroded the influence of the president with the several publics concerned with the university.[9] By yielding to demands of Negro students and granting amnesty to those who occupied the administration building, the faculty may have convinced students that "mass action no matter what it entails is likely to prove effective."[10] Some contend that students engaged in direct protest are right and that faculty support of them against administrative action is justified. At this time however this contention is far from established.

As faculties have concentrated their power over appointment and secured and used extramural funds in departments, as they have created senates with power even over budget preparation, and as they have sided with dissenting students or at least denied support to central administration, they have weakened the ability of presidents to deal with both ordinary and extraordinary administrative problems. The extreme result, and clearly a pathological one, of this process is the black studies division of San Francisco State, which has so much power of self-determination that the central administration can have professors attend meetings only through the threat of withholding salary checks. Even in less pathological situations, faculty assumption of power has been hurtful. At one institution a reform of the undergraduate curriculum was vetoed by departments unwilling to provide needed faculty. At another the deans have lost even the right to do other than formally approve appointments recommended by departments. At still another the faculty tenure committee threatened the president with a confrontation which would require board of trustee intervention unless he accepted, without question, all tenure recommendations the committee wished to make. And at still another institution the faculty is trying to create a new administrative post, that of dean of the faculty. He would be responsible solely to the faculty and would oversee such areas as appointment and tenure. Once again there are those such as John Kenneth Galbraith who believe that

[9] *Ibid.,* p. 118.
[10] *Ibid.,* p. 119.

complete faculty power is the only valid form of academic governance and who to prove the case use the argument that in most of
the prestigious universities, faculties do possess considerable power.
They overlook the fact that, until recently, while faculties had great
independence in some matters, notably their own work, central administration maintained sufficient power over budgets and appointments to govern with some stability. Even Berkeley, which Galbraith
values so highly, gained much of its distinction during the 1950s
and 1960s because the president and chancellors did retain considerable power.

In the matter of the rising cost of higher education, it has
now reached the point at which sources of finance are beginning
to rebel. Some of the increase is caused by needed salary reforms,
rising costs generally, and increased demands made on colleges and
universities. But some at least can be traced to the successful academic revolution and the power faculties have obtained over their
own affairs and the governance of institutions. One can hypothesize
that governance by consensus generally has inflationary tendencies
as each constituency gains support for its demands in return for
support of the desires of others. One can also hypothesize, although
clearly the evidence is not yet available, that increase in cost is
correlated with increase in direct faculty involvement in governance,
whether that be through a senate or a union. Faculties have demanded and received lighter teaching loads at the same time that
the number of courses in the curriculum has been increasing. As
faculty members have obtained extramural support for their research, institutions have been forced to expand tenured faculty just
to maintain essential teaching services. As departments have demanded budgeted funds for research, they have also expected their
number of tenured positions to be increased. All of these changes
add to the cost of higher education, and all could have been limited
by direct monitoring from the center.

This picture is rather bleak. Faculty members have generally
not been very influential in the lives of their students, have not been
particularly innovative, have made governance considerably more
difficult than it need be, have contributed to student protest and

to complicated outcomes of student dissent, and may have contributed to unnecessary increases in the cost of higher education. But there have been some positive results. When led faculties have produced and made work such useful innovations as cluster colleges and cooperative work-study programs. The academic revolution has resulted in such increased capacity to prepare research workers and college teachers that there may even be overproduction. In some institutions a self-restraining faculty has produced a balance of power between itself and the central administration—a balance which allows the institution stable growth. Departmentalism has created such great curricular riches that in a large university a diversity of educational offerings is available to students who want it. However, in balance, academic vices and their implications seem sufficiently overwhelming to demand remedy, but remedy which allows faculties those rights and freedoms essential for their roles as teachers, scholars, and critics.

The most needed reform is a return of legitimate power to the central administration. This reform does not mean a return to the autocratic presidents who ruled their empires with guile and an iron hand. Too many presidents in the past acted without consultation with faculty and sought to implant their own image on their institutions. Rather, if a president is to administer he must have the power to allocate and control financial resources to serve the best interests of the entire university. Only one viewing the total institution can weigh conflicting needs and make decisions among them. The president must also have the power to appoint his own administrative associates. This power probably should extend down to and include department heads because through these associates a president best exerts his administrative leadership. The appointment of deans, for example, should be of as much concern to a president as the appointment of cabinet members is to the President of the United States. Furthermore presidents need the freedom to act, within established policies, in the face of emergency, without fear that they will be subsequently repudiated by their faculties. Thus, when policy is established as to what constitutes intolerable campus disruption, presidents should feel free to act if they have satisfied themselves that those conditions prevail. And a president must maintain a unitary system of administration, in which he alone reports directly to the board of trustees. A dual or multiple system, in which such people as the vice-president for finance and the president of the academic senate report directly to the board, places boards in the role of administration, for which they are unsuited, and makes responsible administration impossible.

A second reform involves tenure. Tenure is an important protection for teachers and scholars, who must deal with controversial ideas in the presence of young and impressionable students who need exposure to controversy but whose parents may wish to shield them from it. As such tenure must be defended. But tenure is not a civil right, granted automatically to all who enter college teaching. It should be earned through demonstration of good judgment, maturity, and competence. An institution should establish, through appropriate processes, that an individual has those particular skills and traits, and tenure should be granted, as a definite act by a board of trustees, only after different people have made appropriate judgments. Members of a department should judge a professor's professional competence and whether departmental needs will best be served through a tenured appointment for one with those skills. Deans should judge whether a recommendation from one department is of comparable quality to recommendations of other departments and in addition whether the school or college wishes to spend the money a tenured appointment entails. A universitywide faculty committee should serve as a quality control group and make the broad judgment of colleagueship—that is, do we want this person as a long time colleague? Then the president must judge whether the institution can afford the quarter to half million dollar investment. For the sake of balanced growth probably no institution should have over 50 per cent of its faculty on tenure, thus ensuring that tenure protects not only the individual but institutional needs for growth as well.

Third, there probably should be a retrenchment in graduate education. If present plans materialize there will be a severe oversupply of holders of Ph.D. and masters degrees by 1980. Estimates run from 50,000 to 100,000 Ph.D.s produced each year by 1980. Many of the evil effects of the academic revolution are traceable to rapid expansion of graduate training and research. This suggestion does not imply a total halt. But developing institutions which plan to enter graduate work in a major way should be discouraged from doing so. Also institutions which already have a large capacity for graduate training should cut back somewhat. Here the lead of the Graduate School of Arts and Sciences at Harvard is setting a good example with its plan to reduce graduate enrollment by 20 per cent by 1975. Without heavy involvement in graduate work college faculties may find the time and inclination to try to improve undergraduate education. Furthermore, less commitment to graduate work may remove some of the invidiousness toward the simple undergraduate college. In states with coordinating boards for higher education the initiative to reduce graduate training could start at that level. In other states and in the private sector the appeal must be made to enlightened self-interest. Colleges and universities simply can no longer afford rapid expansion of graduate programs.

# CHAPTER VI

# Academic Freedom

*A*cademic freedom and tenure have long been considered essential if professors are to do their work effectively. And they still are valid. However, if arrogance and misuse of academic prerogatives persist on the part of academic man, those essential protections will be taken away. What is needed is a new formulation of academic freedom which will account for changed conditions and require a new professorial accountability.

Academic freedom has been claimed by and granted to the academic profession so that its members may properly play their roles for the benefit of the total society. It is a privilege not unlike the sanctity accorded the confessional or the confidentiality granted doctor-patient and lawyer-client relationships. It reflects the high social value of the dignity and worth of the individual. Academic freedom in the United States derives from a number of intellectual traditions, three of which are central: the Western European philosophy of intellectual freedom, the idea of the autonomy of communities of scholars, and the freedoms guaranteed by the federal Bill of Rights. As workable social doctrine academic freedom has evolved slowly as college teachers struggled first against the strictures of dogmatic religions, then against overzealous political control and the rising power of a business community, and, finally, just before codification in generally accepted terms, against presidents and boards of trustees eager to maintain the financial stability and emotional tranquility of the institutions for which they were stewards. An important increment to American formulation of the concept of academic freedom was the German notion of a university as a place in which scholars pursue truth, formulate it, and transmit it to students. However, American academicians added to the German conception a further and critical increment, particularly for the late nineteenth century. They argued that a society would be strengthened by permitting honest condemnation and criticism, and scholars should be privileged to contribute to such a mission. Derivative from this argument is the element of academic freedom which currently gives rise to the most serious criticism of the concept and causes the most difficulty for those who would interpret and practice it. The authors of the 1915 report on academic freedom and academic tenure, instead of limiting academic freedom exclusively to classroom, laboratory, and library, and ensuring institutional neutrality either by requiring a balance of points of view or by prohibiting academics from addressing public issues outside of their own competence, urged the university to disown responsibility for everything its members said or published. As Walter P. Metzger rephrases the resolution, "Academic freedom . . . protects professors in all of their identities—as teachers, scholars, scientists, citizens, experts, consultants—and on every sort of platform. It applies not to a category of speech but to a category of persons."[1]

Since 1915, academic freedom and its shield of permanent tenure have been subjected to many threats, most of which have been reduced or eliminated through decisions on individual cases, modifications of institutional policy and practice, judicial interpretation, and even legislation. Few presidents or boards of trustees would now dream of inquiring whether a professor were espousing orthodoxy in his writings or teaching. Yet at one time this practice seemed defensible. Although court decisions on academic freedom cases have been mixed and although legislation exists and more is frequently urged for demanding theological tests or loyalty oaths to determine student or faculty eligibility to participate in a university, the effectiveness of these strictures in impairing academic freedom appears gradually to be declining. An emerging conventional wisdom was expressed by Chief Justice Earl Warren in his opinion in the case of *Sweezy* v. *New Hampshire:*

> The essentiality of freedom in the community of American universities is almost self-evident. No one should underestimate the vital role in a democracy that is played by those who guide and train our youth. To impose any straitjacket upon the intellectual leaders in our colleges and universities would imperil the future of our nation. No field of education is so thoroughly comprehended by man that new discoveries cannot yet be made. Particularly is that true in the social sciences, where few or any principles are accepted as absolutes. Scholarship cannot flourish in an atmosphere of suspicion and distrust. Teachers and students must always remain free to inquire, to study, and to evaluate, to gain new maturity and understanding. Otherwise, our civilization will stagnate and die.

And leading spokesmen for the AAUP, never Pollyannas about academic freedom, contend:

> Originating as a condition of scholarly endeavor in institutions that performed highly specialized functions, closely related to

[1] W. P. Metzger, *Dimensions of Academic Freedom* (Urbana, Ill.: University of Illinois Press, 1969), p. 6.

philosophy, and restricted until recently to freedoms within those institutions, it has been expanded in the United States to cover faculty members in a great variety of institutions beyond the high school and to protect the liberty to participate in extramural as well as intramural activities. To render this expanded academic freedom secure, impressive professional enforcement machinery has been established, and the law of the land has been evoked to a significant extent.[2]

Although one can be sanguine as to the evolution of academic freedom, serious emerging threats could become operative as public higher education becomes the dominant mode. First, as these institutions increasingly come into the public eye because of cost and centrality to life, with attendant increased temptation for the political arm to intervene in their affairs and to restrict the freedoms of professors, the creation of statewide coordinating commissions and committees for higher education is a contrivance to protect institutions against too great political scrutiny and control while at the same time assuring legislators and the public that their institutions are indeed conducted for the public good and with resources the public can afford. Examples of potential political interference or vindictiveness are legion. The governor of California attempts to use both the powers of his office and his status as a member of boards of trustees to direct state institutions according to his personal convictions, and he publicly favored an action of the Board of Regents which was in direct opposition to a Supreme Court decision. In this case the board used membership in the Communist Party as a criterion for professorial appointment. In the summer of 1969, 131 pieces of legislation introduced at the federal level were aimed at controlling dissent, protest, and violence on the campus; they indicated a sinister proscriptive political intent. The danger was made real when about thirty such laws were passed. The desire of the Illinois state superintendent of public instruction to deny admission to public institutions to students openly espousing

[2] R. F. Fuchs, "Academic Freedom: Its Basic Philosophy Function and History." In L. Joughin (Ed.), *Academic Freedom* (Madison, Wis.: University of Wisconsin Press, 1967), pp. 262–263.

conscientious objection to military service in Viet Nam indicates that politicized members of the educational establishment have coercive tendencies.

Second, of potentially greater significance to academic freedom is the threat of withholding necessary financial support made by legislators, donors, the federal government, and even some of the foundations when institutions and their professors depart too much from orthodoxy. The reality of this threat becomes apparent when communities defeat bond issues because of outrage over faculty statements; when faculty decisions about such for-the-moment controversial matters as ROTC tempt federal agencies to withhold grants and contracts; and when philanthropic foundations feel constrained to deny support for controversial inquiry out of fear of potential strict interpretation of federal regulations governing foundations.

A third threat is of a radically different order, for it appears on the campus itself when dissenting students and faculty members deny essential academic freedom to others out of a sense of the worth of their moral beliefs and a rejection of the beliefs held by others. A threat to academic freedom equally as potent and equally as vindictive as legislative outrage or executive proscription is present when striking students at San Francisco State interrupt and dismiss classes; when bombs are planted at the office doors of faculty members sympathetic to administrative actions; and when faculty members are removed from their offices, as they have been on too many campuses. Max Rafferty, an elected public officer and member of the California Board of Regents, has said, "The same treatment should be meted out to the professors who have been the junior grade fascists—fire them. If some classes have to be closed until some positive-minded instructors can be recruited to take their place—close them." And Mark Rudd, the leader of the Columbia revolt, claimed that "they didn't understand that at times [the student movement] would be impolite about this or intolerant of the other side's rights. . . . They didn't understand that what we did had to be done. We tried to convince them but they sided with the administration." Such statements are destructive to the ideal of academic freedom and are threats to the survival of the concept.

The wonder is that these powerful threats have not been generally employed, with perhaps the major exception of radical student attempts to restrict freedom on the campus. Judged by any standard the American professor enjoys a high degree of academic freedom, and his tenure, when earned, is increasingly guaranteed in written contracts and in public ordinances. However, the professoriate is in serious danger of losing that freedom through certain tendencies within the professoriate itself. If unchecked, they seem bound to release the rage and the proscriptive powers latent in the larger and increasingly disenchanted society. If academic freedom in American colleges and universities is seriously abridged and if the validity of tenure is ultimately denied (as well it could be— legislators in several states have introduced bills to abolish it), these developments are likely to come because of the growing credibility gap concerning the values of higher education and a growing antagonism toward the abuses inflicted by academic man, both individually and collectively. General attacks on academic freedom, if made, will be instigated by irresponsible or unethical actions of professors themselves. These actions will infuriate the rest of society enough to tempt it to withdraw the privilege.

First among these potentially lethal tendencies is what I have described elsewhere in this book as professorial insensitivity to the needs of students. In other self-regulating professions, when insensitivity to clients or patients becomes too rampant, outside agencies have regulated in spite of claimed violation of ancient privilege. Excessive fees charged by medical doctors will probably be limited in Medicare cases through legislation, and courts recently have inclined toward patients in malpractice suits. Perhaps the first salvo in what will become a general attack on academic freedom has been student protest and demand for greater voice in academic governance as the only available and effective way of forcing professors to give them more of their professional and less divided attention.

Then there is the growth of unmonitored consulting and research activities carried on under the protection of academic freedom and free from any save the most superficial public or institutional scrutiny. Some consulting, especially in professional fields, is a desirable way for academic man to test his ideas against reality. And the amount and kind which will be most helpful should be left largely to him to decide. Similarly, wide latitude is necessary in the selection of those research emphases which will best deepen a professor's knowledge of his subject and make him a better instructor. But, when consulting consumes more time than on-campus duties, when research bears no relationship to what is taught, a stronger defense than professorial discretion will likely be called for.

Academic freedom is granted professors solely because the university could not otherwise fulfill its responsibilities to society. The responsibilities consist essentially of training professional people whose skills the society needs, exposing the young to humane values, and searching for truth essential for the achievement of the two previous missions. The privilege is granted so that professors may use recognized and tested techniques in their work. However, in troubled times there has been a marked tendency for some professors to use the tools and techniques of the demigod, the nihilist, or the politician; a professor who uses the sanctity of a classroom to organize his students to take over a university building, a professor who leads a student mob to break and enter university property, and a professor who threatens to grind the institution to a halt unless his version of morality is made into law are but a few examples. Such activities may at times have their place, and certainly the techniques of violence have figured prominently in the history of civilization when other avenues for redress of grievances failed; but indiscriminate use of nonrational approaches to solving difficult human problems (especially if too many problems are attacked at the same time) leads to the suspicion that the academy is not as rational as its spokesmen claim it to be and that perhaps the guarantees to rational inquiry should not be extended to cover violent or destructive behavior. John Millett makes this point eloquently:

## Arrogance on Campus

It would seem that the intellectual tradition would call for social criticism by university faculty members to be voiced in intellectual terms. Certainly the reasoning which underlies any particular economic, political, or social policy and practice deserves critical intellectual scrutiny. . . . It is social criticism divorced from intellectual foundation and it is social criticism as social action which brings conflict between the academic world and the larger society.[3]

During the 1960s American college faculties made major demands for and obtained substantial voice in academic governance; the liturgy for their demands was typically in ideal terms: The faculty is the university, functioning as a community of scholars in the thoughtful search for truth. Only the faculty can judge the qualifications of those who wish to become members. Only the faculty can judge the form and substance of the curriculum; and only the faculty possesses the insight necessary to assess its own performance. This liturgy has been encapsulated in the phrase *shared responsibility,* given currency by the AAHE study of campus governance. The term implies that faculty and administration should be jointly responsible for ensuring that the university achieves its high ideals. Yet the first steps the faculty takes after assuming responsibility seem motivated more by personal economic and welfare concerns than by concern for the educational or research mission of the institution. Listen to one faculty senate.

This is the background out of which the Senate, the new faculty organization, has emerged. It did not come just by accident but for a purpose on which we dare not default. Hence the Senate's most important task for this year is to address itself to specific recommendations to the faculty regarding a faculty personnel policy. A faculty personnel policy includes all the factors in faculty welfare and working conditions: tenure and academic

[3] J. D. Millett, "Value Patterns and Power Conflict in American Higher Education." In *Value Change and Power Conflict in Higher Education* (Berkeley, Calif.: Center for Research and Development in Higher Education, 1969), p. 8.

freedom, appointments and dismissals, rank and salary determinations, work load, professional growth, and evaluation of faculty, sabbaticals, grants and leaves, fringe benefits, and retirement.

Welfare and economic matters are important, but a preoccupation with them implies a relative unconcern for other matters. Such faculty demands for economic gains made under the rubric that they are essential for academic freedom could very well bankrupt institutions in the years ahead. In the past, faculty salaries have been dreadfully inadequate and faculty teaching loads scandalously heavy. But since 1958 institutions have made enormous progress in rectifying poor conditions by increasing tuition and engaging in intensive searches for outside funds. Limits to those sources seem to be rapidly approaching, and yet the demands continue. If they stretch beyond the limits tolerated by reasonable laymen, scrutiny of how funds are expended is sure to follow, and with it monitoring by external agencies. Such monitoring will breach academic freedom.

Expressive in part of this same preoccupation with economic and welfare concerns is the current interest on the part of college faculties in unionism. Academic freedom is an ideal which, when defended in ideal terms and in contexts reasonably free from conflicts of interest or obvious self-serving, has gained and will continue to gain a hearing; but when the ideal is expressed with strong overtones of economic concerns alone, it becomes suspect. The accelerating interest of professors in unionization and in the use of the strike and other economic sanctions has created such a contamination. Strikes are clearly legal and appropriate in a free society, and unions have been of enormous importance in increasing the general welfare. However, strikes and unionization are antithetical to certain ideals clung to by the academic community. Sanford H. Kadish presents the following argument:

> The institutionalization of the collective bargaining strike obscures the special character of a university by regarding it much

as one does any other pluralistic society populated by diverse interest groups and lacking a common commitment to anything more than the bargaining process itself. . . . What is the professor's claim to autonomy, its legitimacy and persuasiveness, . . . is his primary commitment to the service of research and education. To the extent that the professor is prepared to subordinate this service ideal to his employee's self-interest and to relegate the determination of what he is to be accorded to the play of power in a competitive relationship, he has compromised the moral legitimacy of his claim, and the same may be said for other claims such as the claim to academic freedom.[4]

Unionization, collective bargaining, and the strike imply that the services a professor provides can be specified in some detail and listed and can have a definite price placed on them. Academic freedom on the other hand is an open-ended privilege based on the mystique that out of freedom something good will come. Without going into the details of the San Francisco College strike of 1968–1969, I find evidence that public willingness to accord full academic freedom to state college professors was adversely affected because AFT members joined the student strike, which did have a moral base, but focused their own demands around bread-and-butter issues of salaries, work load, grievance procedures, and fringe benefits.

Academic freedom, to remain viable, requires a rule of law and an institution which can be governed. Without these prerequisites anarchy prevails and no rights can long be maintained. However, essential powers to govern, lodged previously in the president, have been so eroded that institutions find themselves impotent in responding to changing conditions. Some of this erosion has been toward systems of institutions; but a great deal of it has been from the president toward faculties organized in departments and to faculty members demanding unmonitored and unregulated perquisites. This trend is especially present in some of the larger, research oriented universities, but increasingly it prevails in even es-

---

[4] S. H. Kadish, *The Strike and the Professional Dimensions of Academic Freedom* (Urbana, Ill.: University of Illinois Press, 1969), pp. 51–55.

sentially teaching institutions. When departmentalized faculties control appointments, the president has lost the power to affect the direction of institutional growth. When the president is denied participation in the process by which tenure is granted until the time for the final acceptance or veto, he is left generally with long-term financial commitments over which he has little control. Yet he is still expected to be responsible for financial stability. Some institutions have gained national publicity because they have developed a participatory style of community governance, and the institutions have seemingly progressed satisfactorily. However, close attention to the dynamics in those institutions reveals an enormous amount of what might be called Machiavellianism on the part of the president, who has been forced to govern through guile rather than through legitimate exercise of responsible authority. Talent for Machiavellian manipulation, however, is probably not widespread in college and university administrators. Hence, to remove responsible authority from a president seems likely to ensure no governance, which in turn places the freedom of any one faculty member or group of faculty members at the mercy of competitive academic forces.

A brief digression may make my point. The president of one Midwestern institution recognized for community governance has a reputation of generally being allied with students against faculty syndicalism. Substituting just a few words in a portion of Machiavelli's chapter "Of the Civic Principality" describes governance at that institution.

> The students, on the other hand, when unable to resist the faculty, endeavor to exalt and create a president in order to be protected by his authority. He who becomes president by help of the faculty has greater difficulty in maintaining his power than he who is raised by the students, for he is surrounded by those who think themselves his equal and is thus unable to direct or command as he pleases. But one who is raised to the presidency by students finds himself alone and has no one, or very few, who are not ready to obey him. Besides which, it is impossible to satisfy the faculty by fair dealing and without inflict-

ing injury on others, whereas it is very easy to satisfy the mass of the students in this way, for the aim of the students is more honest than that of the faculty, the latter desiring to oppress and the former merely to avoid oppression.

Machiavelli goes on to describe how the president should deal with the faculty.

I would say that the faculty are to be considered in two different manners. That is, they are to be ruled either so as to make them entirely dependent on your fortunes or else not. Those that are thus bound to you and are not rapacious must be honored and loved. Those who stand aloof must be considered in two ways. Either they do this through pusillanimity and natural want of courage; and in this case you want to make use of them, and especially such as are of good counsel, so that they may honor you in prosperity and in adversity you have not to fear them. But when they are not bound to you of set purpose and for ambitious ends, it is a sign that they think more of themselves than of you, and from such men the president must guard himself and look upon them as secret enemies who will help to rule him when in adversity.

The last of this particular list of tendencies, although it is by no means exhaustive, is the inclination of faculty to emphasize its prerogatives, its economic well-being and welfare, and its interests without recognizing institutional rights. This tendency is exemplified in different ways, but perhaps in one way more clearly than in others: the rigid insistence that institutions comply with AAUP policy regarding probation before the granting of tenure. If one examines the 1940 policy in the context of the 1940s, it is eminently reasonable and is intended to accomplish good. It states in essence that seven years' total probationary experience at all institutions served should be sufficient evidence upon which to grant tenure, with the proviso that regardless of previous length of service a given institution may require up to four years of probationary experience. At the end of that time, in the absence of any definite act on the part of the administration, the faculty member is presumed to have achieved permanent tenure. In the 1940s, relatively few institutions had developed tenure policies, and, particularly in a number of liberal arts colleges and teachers colleges (they had not yet emerged as state universities), the spirit of the old public school system seemed to prevail. In this view there was probably something morally wrong with a faculty member spending too long at a given post. The prototype of institutions at that time was a California college whose faculty members were discouraged from purchasing homes on the ground that they became too deeply entrenched. Those conditions have changed. Most institutions have finally developed definite policy statements, and, in a number of states, laws ensure tenure for professors at public institutions (particularly state colleges and junior colleges) at the end of a stipulated period of time. Increasingly, the probationary period tends to be three years or under for all save the completely inexperienced teacher.[5] This change has had two effects which are potentially antithetical to academic freedom. First, if the three-year probationary period is mandated by law and if the procedures for terminating appointments include not only institutional due process but judicial review, the administration is forced to begin to accumulate evidence against a professor from the first moment of service, just in case a negative decision for appointment is subsequently made and the institution is called into court to defend its action. Second, and this applies with peculiar poignancy to private institutions depending on tuition for basic operating expenses, rigorous demands for early tenure decision face them with an unfortunate dilemma. Either they must accept a very high faculty turnover with the attendant drop in overall faculty morale as they seek to make decisions before faculty members drift into tenure, or they must allow a disproportionate percentage of their faculty to have permanent tenure, thus committing heavy financial resources when the availability of these resources is by no means assured.

These tendencies may not prove lethal but the press and administrators and governing boards suggest they probably will. A

[5] AAUP, while not changing its policy, has gone on record as supporting a definite statement of reasons before a nontenured faculty member may be discharged. Thus the net effect here is to shorten the time served.

**105**

better safeguard than sheer hope would be a revised theory of academic freedom which would support the public good and which would attract the necessary endorsement of the larger society. This new theory would encompass much which has evolved since the 1915 declaration of principles but should also deal directly and explicitly with other matters. First, such a theory must assume that there are behaviors which academic freedom does not protect or ensure. Academic freedom does not protect a professor from several kinds of accountability, the easiest of which to accept is accountability to individual peers as professionals. But scholars are also accountable to their colleagues in a corporate sense because the irresponsible acts of a few endanger the intellectual freedom of all. This point seems particularly appropriate for radical faculty members to consider, for their pursuit of their own morally determined goals by techniques other than those of the university could very well jeopardize freedom for all. Then, too, faculty members are accountable to their students, and academic freedom can never be presumed to protect exploiting or ignoring students' needs and desires. Too many faculty members have insisted on their own academic freedom but have been careless about the freedom of students; and too frequently teachers have circumscribed student rights to question, criticize, or dissent. Disregard for this accountability should be a basis for genuine disciplinary action. Two other sorts of accountability should be briefly mentioned. There must be some fundamental sense in which faculty members are accountable to their institution, its purposes, goals, and survival, so that acts detrimental in any fundamental way to the institution are proscribed. And academic freedom does not protect against public accountability, regardless of whether the professor serves in a privately or publicly controlled institution. Both are in the final analysis agencies of service to the society, and he who serves them must serve society.[6]

Second, academic freedom cannot be considered as protection against evaluation and judgment of performance, including administrative assessment. Regardless of how casually or systemati-

[6] This notion of accountability is derived from T. R. McConnell, "Faculty Interests in Value Change and Power Conflict." In *Value Change and Power Conflict, op. cit.,* pp. 57–73.

cally it is done, evaluation and judgment of professional worth are constantly being made. However, assessment should be more precisely, objectively, and rigorously attempted than it now is. It could even include administrative consideration of student evaluation of faculty and critical examination of the time faculty members devote to the various professional tasks which confront them. In principle there probably is very little argument against this point, yet increasingly faculty members resist evaluation once they have acquired the protection of tenure, and they insist on only limited evaluation done exclusively by peers before that time.

Third, and this is quite a touchy matter, academic freedom is not designed as protection against the consequences of one's own actions, particularly when those actions are prohibited by law. Thus the professors at San Francisco State College who went out on strike in 1969 in violation of state law and whose tenured appointments were terminated after due process may very well complain about misfortune but cannot complain that their academic freedom has been violated. Some striking teachers who did so in the face of legal prohibition were reinstated, but this fact is more the product of the intervention of overwhelming political power than of interpretation of the concept of academic freedom.

Fourth, another sort of behavior, also difficult to express, which nonetheless would appear to have some validity is that academic freedom should not be a protection against punishment for crimes committed against an institution. These crimes must be carefully defined and specified, but possible examples are destroying or leading students to destroy university property, physically assaulting officers of the institution or publicly vilifying officers or colleagues, and physically harming, insulting, or humiliating visitors to the campus to such an extent that the professor would be liable in the courts. Some would argue that the civil and criminal laws are sufficient for such actions and the institution, therefore, should not take cognizance of them. However, if the professor is indeed responsible to his institution, a reasonable extension of this principle would allow an institution operating through its forms of due process to apply sanctions up to and including termination.

These elements of this enlarged theory of academic freedom

are largely negative, pointing out activities which academic freedom does not protect. But there are some positive elements as well. Many of the efforts to define academic freedom and to strengthen tenure protect the professor almost on the assumption that he automatically will fulfill ethically his responsibilities as a teacher and scholar. Some insurance is provided through the system by which research and scholarship are published and reviewed; but no similar restraints exist with respect to professorial relationships with students. No carefully developed set of ethical criteria focuses on the role of the professor as a member of a helping profession, and quite obviously no sanctions are available to ensure such appropriate conduct. But they should be available. Just as the AAUP stands ready to investigate alleged violations of the academic freedom of professors, so there should be mechanisms to investigate and apply sanctions when the freedoms of and obligations owed students are violated or unfulfilled. Several professional associations have joined together in making broad statements concerning human rights. These, however, have the sanction only of persuasion, and the AAUP has found that something other than persuasion is all too frequently needed.

Then, too, a revised theory of academic freedom should speak to the needs and to the protection of administrative officers who must deal with controversy, who are responsible for the education of youth, and who are subject to even more strenuous pressures than professors are. For too long academic freedom and tenure have been the exclusive rights of individuals holding academic rank and engaging in teaching and research. In some way, protection other than the goodwill of a board of trustees should be afforded administrative officers speaking out on the issues of concern to society. Perhaps if such protection could be contrived, presidential utterances might be less banal than they now frequently appear to be.

This enlarged conception of academic freedom needs also to stress professorial self-restraint, in regard to both professional and personal activities. Having defended several score academic freedom cases over the last quarter century, I have always been struck by how frequently the case might not have arisen, and with no loss of essential freedom, had the professor exercised self-restraint and discretion. One who believes in the freedom of a professor to organize his courses as he sees fit had to, as a matter of principle, support the young faculty members at the University of California, Berkeley, who invited Eldridge Cleaver to deliver a majority of the lectures in their course. Yet, in another way, inviting Cleaver could be judged as deliberate provocation for a confrontation with the Board of Regents when none was needed. It is of questionable ethics for professors to use the concept of academic freedom to illegally attempt to assume power over a university. The Board of Regents of the University of California has frequently acted misguidedly and has been challenged a number of times by the faculty senate over the issue of control. Until now, the regents have succeeded in defeating every major attack and seem likely to do so in the future, perhaps because academic freedom is a concept ill suited for the raw politics of power.

# CHAPTER VII

---

# *New Patterns*

---

The distortion and misuse of endemic academic traits and privileges have led colleges and universities to be unresponsive to emerging social needs. The needs are all plain to see: education of the disadvantaged, repair of urban blight, scholarly and effective criticism of society, and educationally based service to many different groups. But instead of providing these needs institutions and their professors have become narrowly preoccupied with graduate training and research, leaving the larger tasks unattended.

# New Patterns

Left to their own devices and without the spur of outside criticism and coercion, American colleges and universities can generally be expected to fail to perform those functions for which society provides support and for which academic man claims special privileges. There are exceptions. A few colleges, without knowing how, have left generations of students profoundly different. Here and there, a professor, largely through the force of his own personality, has influenced and moved all who have come in contact with him. But in the majority of the 2,300 institutions, conducted by some 500,000 faculty, students enter and leave and seem to grow not much more than they would had the time been spent in war, work, or on welfare. James Trent observed, after studying a good cross-section, that college graduates "could be judged largely apathetic to intellectual inquiry and social issues," and established that those college students who did grow in autonomy came "as a group from relatively more autonomous and educationally oriented families."[1] Andrew Greeley discovered that alumni, several years after graduation, liked their colleges but not too much and revealed little, if any, active interest in intellectual or artistic matters.[2]

The catalog of errors is easy to present. The curriculum is the formal arrangement of courses and experiences through which the college seeks to achieve the educational goals it sets for itself. And since faculty salaries constitute a large part of a budget, the curriculum is the most expensive technique used to effect change. Yet students testify that friendships and out-of-class experiences affect them most, and only a minority claim to have any significant interest in academic matters. Joseph Katz showed that even in such academically pretentious institutions as Stanford and Berkeley only "about one-fourth said that ideas prescribed in courses by teachers had much influence"[3] and Kenneth Keniston discovered that

[1] J. W. Trent and L. L. Medsker, *Beyond High School: A Study of 10,000 High School Students* (San Francisco: Jossey-Bass, 1968), p. 232.

[2] A. M. Greeley, unpublished report to the Carnegie Commission on Higher Education, 1969.

[3] J. Katz and Associates, *No Time for Youth: Growth and Constraint in College Students* (San Francisco: Jossey-Bass, 1967), p. 15.

**111**

young radical students, although able, and frequently from intellectual homes, "began to scorn the ease with which they could get good grades, and a number decided that classroom work was largely irrelevant to their real education."[4] The explanation for these criticisms is that college courses are subdivisions of information of personal and financial concern to faculty members, who tend to believe that what preoccupies them should excite others. This self-centeredness is cloaked with such rationalizations as "every student should understand the broad outlines of human knowledge" or "only through exposure to the great thoughts of the Western tradition can students acquire greatness of spirit." But, in essence, college courses are as they are because they appeal to the logic of a professor, or at least to the logic of a professor who wrote a textbook, and are conducted without thought as to whether they appeal to students. Only self-interest could delude professors into believing that one or two years' instruction in a foreign language can develop insight into the nature of either a language or a foreign culture or that a survey of excerpts from classical writers can create an affinity for the Greeks.

Then there is the treatment of students. Although the analogy that "the student is a nigger" is overdrawn, college teachers do manifest, if not a dislike, certainly a lack of respect for students and their developmental needs. There is too much truth in the professorial aphorism that a college would be a wonderful place were it not for the students. Grades are important in the lives of students, yet college grading, in all save the few institutions which have developed large scale testing programs, is unreliable, capricious, and based more on professorial hunch than on rational efforts to be objective. When the market for college teachers allowed, there was a flight from teaching and a quest for a one- or at the most two-course load so that professors could get on with their own work. Office hours are kept to a minimum, and despite student testimony and evidence as to the change which can come from a close relationship between professor and student, professors cling to their

[4] K. Keniston, *Young Radicals* (New York: Harcourt, Brace, and World, 1968), p. 88.

own and seem afraid of counseling students. There is a strong suspicion that professors frequently exploit students to satisfy their psychological needs for a disciple, an audience, a scapegoat, or an idolater. How else can we explain the skepticism regarding credit based on examination or the reluctance to abandon attendance requirements? And possibly some professorial rage at students' inadequate use of language, failure to read broadly, and lack of cultural interests is a sublimated admission that they share in those vices.

One of the major arguments for academic freedom, tenure, and the freedom of the university is that higher education has been constituted as a critic of the society. And the ideal is worthy. But, in practice, those in higher education have not performed this role. Generally, educational leaders have not been those who encouraged social change. Instead they have simply codified accepted belief and made it their ideological credo. Their public utterances, with a few notable exceptions, do not deal with critical social problems unless those problems impinge directly on the immediate concerns of higher education. Little academic concern was expressed about the draft until revision of the law threatened graduate enrollments, and even then the outcry was delayed six months after the change in law was made. Few university presidents, professors, or educational organizations took public stands on the inequities of a segregated society until galvanized to do so by the efforts of Negro ministers, working people, and college students. A nonacademic writer warned about the dangers of pesticides, and another declared that automobiles were unsafe. Simply to illustrate, a collection of one college president's speeches is described on the dust jacket as coming to grips with some of the major political, socioeconomic, and moral issues of our time, yet the sixteen item table of contents reveals only one title which does not deal explicitly with the professional concerns of higher education, and that one, in content, is also so concerned.[5] Some academics joined in the civil rights effort,

---

[5] H. D. Gideonse, *Against the Running Tide* (New York: Twayne, 1967).

conservation causes, protests against the war in Viet Nam, and political action, most notably in support of Eugene McCarthy. But their numbers were relatively few and their timing was poor. They followed a lead set by other parts of the society.

It can be argued that social criticism, which higher education should provide, is of a different order than other endeavors and is expressed through scholarly analyses of social disorders. The analyses gradually are popularized and filter into public conversation and social discussion. But, unfortunately, even this does not happen. Much of the research in the social and behavioral sciences has been reactive to the availability of funds initiated outside of the academy rather than designed to deal with critical issues on the ground that then support can be found. Considerable research in 1969 concerned the education of the disadvantaged, while major research effort in the 1950s had to do with mental retardation. The variable which accounts best for this shift is the availability of support by the federal government or some of the larger foundations reinforced by wide public awareness that a problem exists.

Somewhat related is the need to find ways to educate segments of the population previously judged ineducable. In 1967, the facts about Negro educational needs were reasonably well known, as was the fact that despite impressive gains in civil rights, Negroes were educationally and economically worse off than they were at the start of the civil rights movement. Evidence from studies, frequently conducted outside of the university, also showed that changed educational environment could bring impressive gains in the educational levels and the achievement of Negro students. Yet colleges and universities continued to do business as usual, trying to become selective along the limited dimension of measured or demonstrated academic aptitude and accepting the fact that few Negro, Mexican-American, or Indian students could meet established standards of admission. Some institutions had begun to talk about helping high risk students but with no sense of urgency. The death of Martin Luther King, Jr., stimulated black student unions to demand increased educational opportunity—a demand which could no longer be resisted because of long term institutional

114

vulnerability and a finally awakened academic conscience. Since that tragic assassination, institutions have begun various programs and experiments. Still, however, the attempts are not examples of the application of disciplined intelligence to problems. If they were, something more than reduced course load, available guidance, and precollege summer sessions in which to study mathematics and English would generally be found. New programs appear to have no relationship to the insights gained in the behavioral sciences.

The university also should be concerned with and respond to the problems of the urban condition, which has come to be the prevailing life style of the United States. Gradually, people have become aware of what is happening—that most Americans are living or will live in large metropolitan areas. And they also feel that colleges and universities should do something about urban problems. They have in mind the model of land grant colleges helping to revolutionize American agriculture and the quality of rural life (given some assist by noneducational provision of low cost electrical power). But there the matter still sits. There are claims for urban grant universities, there are a few centers for urban studies, and there is much discussion of what can be done about urban problems. Faculties of institutions specifically enjoined to serve urban communities reject the idea of service and turn instead to orthodox theoretical studies. Junior colleges are located in the suburbs, away from the central city, and extension programs are mounted and maintained only if they can be self-supporting and not a drain on institutional resources.

This catalog could be extended. Technology has produced television, sound tapes, films, radios, computers, inexpensive processes for reproduction of visual materials, and relatively inexpensive transportation—all of which have powerful implications for education. Yet most education is conducted in ways which equally frequently could have been found in the 1890s or in the thirteenth century. The universities and colleges are social institutions which could and should be studied intensively in order to improve. Yet, for the most part, scholars seek objectivity when studying other phenomena but rely on intuition and limited personal experience to understand the university. Few scholars in history, political science, psychology, and related disciplines direct their full attention to higher education, and the void has been filled by nonhistorians who write the history of education and mathematicians who study improvement of teaching. Sven Lundstedt edited a series of papers dealing with higher education in social psychology, but nowhere in the book are data about how programs function or even about application of social psychological theory to educational problems.[6] Yet one would presume that such areas as role theory might be germane.

Finally, during the late 1950s and through the 1960s higher education attained the highest public regard and the highest levels of public support of any time since the founding of Harvard. But by 1969 a credibility gap of serious dimensions had emerged. Spokesmen for higher education had claimed and promised too much and delivered too little. Even in medical research it is clear that "science . . . can no longer hope to exist, among all human enterprises, through some mystique, without constraints or scrutiny in terms of national goals, and isolated from the competition for allocation of resources which are finite . . . unless we biomedical scientists are prepared to examine our endeavors, our objectives, and our priorities, and to state our case openly and clearly, the future will be different indeed."[7]

If these charges are valid, the question remains: Can conditions be remedied? Can colleges and universities and the organizations and associations within which they operate accept the fact of failure and make the moral decision to correct errors? In the past reform has usually come only when institutions were faced with mortal danger and had to change or die. Liberal arts colleges in the mid-nineteenth century are examples. If the alternatives for higher education today are phrased strongly enough, as they should be, perhaps the threats will again bring change. Unless the curriculum

---

[6] S. Lundstedt, *Higher Education in Social Psychology* (Cleveland: Press of Case Western Reserve University, 1968).

[7] I. L. Bennett as quoted in D. S. Greenberg, *The Politics of Pure Science* (New York: New American Library, 1967), p. 287.

and teaching are improved, presently alienated youth could in desperation destroy the concept of a university. If institutions do not sustain their recently acquired concern for Negroes, black militancy and separation could bring higher education to a halt. And if higher education does not concern itself directly with urban problems, some other agency will.

Several paths toward rectification seem possible. The first, as mentioned previously, is to reassess the role of research in colleges and universities. In the majority of colleges and universities the principal obligation should be to teaching, and faculty pressures to engage in supported research should be resisted, as should the struggle of predominantly teaching institutions to become graduate and research oriented universities. Even in the major research universities some retrenchment is in order. Big science research probably should be concentrated in separate research institutes rather than in universities, where the sheer budget for such activities distorts the emphasis of the entire university. And even in major universities we can wonder if the assumption that all professors are doing productive research is warranted. A casual glance at annual reports reveals textbook writing, conference participation, and polemical writing as the chief results of research. These are not bad activities. But should tuition or the appropriations made for the education of undergraduates subsidize them? The counterargument accepts waste and ineffectual scholarly activities on the ground that such freedom also leads to the discoveries which modify human life. But some control is essential; some judgments should be made about the activities of professors, hopefully by universities, for if they do not, society will make the judgments and exercise the control.

This step can be taken only as part of a larger effort, that of reordering priorities and cutting away some activities which are no longer productive or which are inconsistent with institutional purposes, conceived of as parsimoniously possible. For most collegiate institutions the order should be education first, then educationally based service, and last, and quite least, research. Whether the mission be the production of associate of arts, bachelors, or master's degree holders, the emphasis should be on teaching those candidates as effectively as possible. And even in those institutions which rightfully are charged with doctoral work, attention should be given to the curriculum students follow, to advising them, and to organizing educational experiences which reasonably might be expected to produce teacher-scholars. The American Ph.D. is highly regarded, but this regard quite possibly is in spite of the quite casual way doctoral instruction is offered rather than because of it. Consider the disjointed conversations which are classed as graduate seminars, or the oral examinations in defense of theses unread by the examiners, or the theses themselves which, at least in some of the verbal fields, are more confused and confusing jargon than examples of reflective thought about a subject of intrinsic significance.

As part of this reordering of priorities considerable attention should be given to admission processes. High selectivity along the dimension of academic aptitude or previous academic performance is only a recent phenomenon. There is no evidence that the products of highly selective institutions are any more productive as human beings, as scholars, or as intellectuals than were those products of an earlier, less competitive time. Since academic aptitude and previous academic performance predict only future academic performance, which increasingly appears unrelated to subsequent success, institutions could, if they chose, modify admission practices. For institutions where space is limited, random selection of those who apply could be used and with little if any adverse effect, for students do apply to institutions in which they believe they will be comfortable. Furthermore a random technique would ensure that minority group applicants would be evenly represented. As for other institutions not bothered by an oversupply of applicants, return to the simple criterion of high school graduation would not only conform to facts but, as a by-product, would save countless agonized hours of admission committees.

Important among these paths to reformation is the need for institutional honesty and candor about all activities. Honesty not only might be revealing for institutions but also might provide a base for restoration of public faith in higher education. Consider these questions. To what extent is the cost of instruction for lower division students so substantially below that for upper division students as to constitute a subsidy? To what extent are state support formulas for graduate work, which assume perhaps a one to four student-teacher ratio, at variance with the reality of seminars composed of twenty or thirty students, with the surplus funds being used to support faculty research even if trivial? To what extent is the generally high attrition rate in colleges and universities a reflection of student disenchantment rather than the product of demanding standards vigorously and objectively imposed? What are the admission standards an institution applies as distinguished from those released for public consumption? For what vocations can an institution reasonably prepare students if candid criteria are applied? The way these questions are phrased reveals a belief that institutions have all too frequently been if not dishonest certainly a bit misleading.

A related need is for realistic claims and objectives for collegiate institutions. Colleges and universities cannot do all the things their catalogs say they do. Liberal arts colleges cannot prepare for the number of vocations implied by the various professional and preprofessional curricula listed. Graduate schools of education with existing resources cannot prepare the many different specialists they claim the profession needs, nor can schools of business, journalism, librarianship, or social work. Junior colleges cannot offer the intimate counseling they claim to provide with the size faculty their resources allow. Nor can a program of general education produce people with a deep awareness of science, a mature set of values, an appreciation for the great and the beautiful, and a lifetime devotion to learning. Colleges and universities are well designed to do a few things. They can occupy the time of late adolescents until the work force is ready for them. They can develop or improve language and number skills. They can provide some time for the young to think about themselves and who they are. They can instill a limited amount of generally needed information to enable people to communicate with each other. They can create opportunities for young people of the same age group to interact with each other. They

**119**

can train some students in the particular skills needed in some vocations, but by no means all or even a majority. And these are all worthy functions and are quite properly the reason for the existence of an institution.

The last path to reform is based on the assumption that as human beings develop and change, they need different kinds of assistance. Thus parents can provide one sort of assistance and a church another. College students have certain developmental needs to which they expect colleges to respond. They need to transfer some feelings about parents to other adults. They need help in understanding and using emotions. They need guidance as to what the world of work is all about. They need to learn to live in a small group not their family and to cooperate with others. These few examples indicate that the undergraduate college should occupy itself with meeting those developmental needs of undergraduates which it is qualified to meet, and that the faculty should see itself and the curriculum as existing first and foremost for that purpose.

If these paths were followed, a new yet old pattern of American higher education would emerge. The headlong rush of institutions to enter graduate education and sponsored research would be curtailed. It is possible to envision higher educational systems in which most institutions concern themselves with the education of undergraduate students or advanced undergraduates who receive a masters degree with no implication of any particular research competence. A limited number of institutions would offer the various doctoral degrees which the society needs. But these institutions would concentrate their energies and resources on the production of those degree-holders, and research would be specifically designed to facilitate doctoral student training; hopefully faculty interests would not be antithetical to such a purpose. Large contract research, of the order that presently distorts institutional budgets, would not be fostered or encouraged. If the profit and largess which contract research provides for university professors were eliminated, other institutions would not be quite so intrigued with entering the terribly expensive domain of advanced graduate education. Furthermore, if contract research were minimized in uni-

120

versities, one important source of student discontent would be eliminated—that of defense and war related research. The university preoccupation with research independent of its educational mission seems likely to be eliminated by many forces and factors. The suggestion offered here could enable higher education to make the change in good grace and with autonomy, rather than to make forced changes which might also affect adversely delicate educational decisions.

A modification of the entire system of higher education should also result in a curtailment of spiraling costs. Such curtailment would have significance, especially for private institutions, which are experiencing a crisis that could force many out of existence. Private tuitions increased almost yearly as institutions sought to recruit faculty in a competitive market. Some of this competition resulted from a shortage of the teaching faculty needed to cope with unprecedented and unexpected demands for college education. But that supply-demand problem was aggravated by the reduction in teaching loads which accompanied the increase in university based research. There are several strands to this issue. As a device to recruit faculty, the reduced teaching load, paid for by contract research funds, became the rule. To compete, liberal arts colleges had to decrease teaching loads and at the same time increase course offerings if they were to compete for the best students, or so they believed. Within universities increases in research activity meant that more faculty had to be recruited, and, given the competitive climate, the universities had to make more long term commitments in the form of tenured appointments. A few institutions— or at least one—have taken the conservative stance of appointing to tenure only those professors for whom there are endowed funds. Most, however, have lived dangerously and have expanded their faculties on the assumption that the research grants as well as the stock market would rise indefinitely. This metaphor is apt, for in a rising market stock frequently becomes inflated out of proportion to the true earning capacity of a company, but that very inflation stimulates still further price rises. A general diminishing of research would lower costs and allow private institutions to return to financial stability and to continue to provide a reasonable share of the collegiate education needed. Thus the precipitous decrease in the proportion of young people educated by private higher education could be slowed, and private higher education could once again set styles and modes for education which could be emulated in the public sector.

Once again, events are likely to move in this direction without reference to argument as a result of somewhat impersonal forces. The overall expansion of capacity for advanced graduate students which has taken place since about 1955 is now producing so many potential college teachers that there may be an oversupply by the mid-1970s. In some fields there are already more new Ph.D.s than there are positions. Of course as supply and demand come into balance this will affect not only salary levels but even the compulsion some institutions feel to cater to the demands for light teaching loads and research opportunities.

The third element in this new fabric derives logically from the first two. With concentration on teaching and on education the chief business of most institutions, faculties can turn their attention to problems of the curriculum and to the needs of students. This does not mean a move toward utopia. College faculty members are mortal, quite human, and far from perfect. But without the implied demand that most faculty members do research, latent interests on the part of at least some professors in teaching and education can be released, and probably enough have such interests for a new tone to emerge. If, in most four year institutions, faculty members did not feel obliged to seek a grant, join the jet set, or become cosmopolitans, they might have more time for their students and their courses. In the graduate universities as well, without the pressure to secure outside support for their research in order to ease the financial strain on normal institutional funds, professors might attend to their graduate students and those research activities needed for their training. This argument, it should be recognized, flies in the face of what conventional wisdom calls greatness or excellence in higher education—a community of scholars, setting their own tasks for the production of knowledge, in the company, where appropriate, of younger scholars, their students. That ideal does have charm, and the life is nice. It is, however, unrealistic. States and private donors will not for long tolerate teaching loads so low that an average of one or two courses is the rule to the end that the professor may conduct his research without reference to social needs and is satisfied if, by serendipity, a few students are stimulated to pattern themselves after their mentor.

# Chapter VIII

# New Academic Morality

B̲efore faculties can reform themselves and their academic values, a new academic morality must be contrived. That new morality must be based on a concept of teaching as a helping profession in which the professional gives of himself for the good of others. The crises on the campus derive fundamentally from unresolved moral dilemmas and perplexities. People in quandary, daily facing urgent but seemingly unsolvable problems, tend to act, often irrationally, for the pure catharsis which action brings. Until those uncertainties are resolved the pattern of irrational action continues. Their resolution, however, requires first their identification, then understanding how they emerged, and finally a context congenial to the creation of new and appropriate moral standards.

People on campus have no appropriate guide lines or criteria by which to govern personal conduct. The highly restrictive proscriptions based upon Christian or Jewish orthodoxy are no longer appropriate; yet nothing has replaced those canons. Student sexual behavior, for example, is freer than previously yet neither the majority of students nor those responsible have been able or willing to replace the old "thou shall not" with "thou shall," and the compromise "that sexual behavior must be considered in a total context" proves unsatisfying and elusive. Professors, tempted by the requests of a society needing professional services, have undertaken to serve many masters but with no true sense as to how to decide among conflicting demands on their time. When requests for specified research or consulting were not made, as was generally true before World War II, there was no issue. Professors served their students and their institutions. But with concurrent demands to teach students, to advise government on policy, and to conduct research which might lead to world peace or a cure for cancer, professors need but do not have help in ordering priorities. Similarly, at one time, people knew what behaviors were expected of students, teachers, and administration. Roles were fulfilled because time and conditions provided the necessary stability. But high mobility and changing characteristics of groups on campus have created conditions antithetical to easy role fulfillment. Thus people, not knowing who they are, do not have standards for behavior.

For many reasons the democratic ideal of personal freedom has encountered the contrary ideal of social good. This conflict has never been absent, but conditions on college and university campuses in the postwar decades have sharpened the tension. The older ideal of academic freedom grants the scholar the right to pursue his own research free from all restrictions save those of his own abilities. Yet exercise of such freedom may violate institutional, social, or personal priorities of others. Should scholars be allowed to work on nerve gas, problems of oil production, or ethnic differences in intelligence if those matters violate social conscience or institutional viability? The concept of academic freedom also neither anticipates nor accommodates a politicized campus. It provides no help on such an issue as violence on the campus in pursuit of moral but personal aims. Similarly, at one time institutions felt free to use their resources of land and money to achieve the limited objectives specified in their charters. But as community needs impinged on the campus, as they did at Columbia and Chicago, or as counterclaims for institutional finances were urgently advanced, as were those of Negro children living in nearby ghettos, irrepressible and perhaps irreconcilable conflict resulted.

Another dilemma, also rooted in democratic ideals, is the conflict between elitism, seemingly essential in a society based on merit, and equality of opportunity. Presently this conflict is manifest in the debate over the use of open college admissions as one way of rectifying ancient abuse. But to admit to college large numbers of inadequately prepared students ignores long accepted standards and very likely penalizes other, perhaps better prepared students. If the capacity of an institution is limited, how does it decide whether, on one hand, to accept 10 per cent of a freshman class from disadvantaged groups in full awareness that survival rates will be low or standards will be changed or, on the other hand, to adhere to a thousand year old mission of accepting and preparing those most qualified to enter professional and leadership roles? This conflict is experienced most strikingly in private institutions which depend on tuition paid by students. If they use these funds for those who pay them they ignore a major social problem, yet if they attend seriously to disadvantaged people, they jeopardize their existence. And institutional souls are not saved through losing their lives.

A different conflict involves the essential role of the scholar, whether teacher or student. The ideal is that the scholar is granted his privilege of academic freedom so that he may pursue truth in tranquility through the exercise of reason. Thus the scholar is most true to himself when he detaches himself from the pressing and the immediate for the sake of a larger vision. Students accordingly are most true to themselves when they prepare, through disciplined but detached study, for the time when they will be able to act. But such remoteness, in the presence of critical social problems, leads to charges of irrelevance and insensitivity. Scholars, runs the counter-argument, must act on issues of war, race, or environment or else stand accused, as were the German professors, of indifference. Yet, if scholars leave their libraries and laboratories, what of the preservation and advancement of culture? Men tolerated medieval monks and eventually venerated them for the preservation of civilization. Their modern counterparts seemingly are allowed no such easy choice.

Another moral conflict is that between the rule of law, which by its very nature works slowly, and the pressure to solve problems which appear to have emerged overnight. (The fact that they have not is immaterial.) Universities have evolved slowly, and along with positive attributes they have also developed hurtful traits and insensitivities. Admissions policies have hardened stratification in a society which prides itself on being open. Institutional growth has taken land from the tax rolls and from disadvantaged peoples. Institutional investment policy has contributed to at one time profitable war based industry. And institutions have become related to big government, big business, and even big labor, so that, in a sense, they constitute a closed corporation. To some the human inequities thus engendered—ghettos existing in the shadows of the Gothic, humane letters nurturing and tutoring the military, and depersonalized educational practices assuring economic stability—are so abhorrent that they must be eliminated at once and by violence if needed. Violence on the campus seems less oppressive than the violence of imposed disadvantage or the violence of an unpopular war. To those so inclined, the rule of law is too slow, yet to end the rule of law eventually jeopardizes the freedom of all and the essential nature of a university.

# Arrogance on Campus

A dilemma difficult to express but nonetheless real involves the relationships between students and professors. In the past a student was not compelled to subject himself to the tuition of a professor. Rather through a moral decision he read books, wrote papers, and conducted exercises assigned in the faith that these would help him develop in ways he wished. If he thought otherwise, he had the right to leave. But as social organization placed a premium on college experience and made college education the chief means of social mobility, the freedom within which moral decisions could be exercised eroded. Students who felt forced to attend classes also felt it proper to make demands and to have a voice in shaping their experiences. This feeling is seen clearly in student demands for their own curricula tailored to meet their interests as they see them. Society may compel them to be in school, and it may compel them to acquire a degree, but it has no right to compel them to submit to what they consider drudgery. What once was a moral relationship has become an adversary one governed by the interplay of power blocs. Neither students nor professors are prepared for and ways have not been institutionalized to accommodate the new relationships. Thus, pure awkwardness leads to confrontation.

Finally, as social demands are placed on colleges and universities for more services to be provided with limited resources, the ordering of priorities becomes critical. Yet the decisions are unlike those which may be made on the basis of profit or loss, military victory, or evidenced public utility. They are moral decisions which must be made without moral guide lines or criteria. How does an institution decide to eliminate speech and drama rather than biological science? How long should a private institution continue to produce desperately needed medical doctors if by doing so the vitality of work in literature or art is sapped? Which should be stressed, a vigorous, vital, but costly undergraduate program or a thrust into graduate work and research? What responsibility does a university have to preserve the study of classics when funds thus used could be put to the service of preparing teachers of the disadvantaged? Frequently such decisions have been made expediently.

# New Academic Morality

Availability of outside funds dictates physical science over journalism. But expedient decisions are vulnerable to moral attack as well as to reversals through changes in internal forces and factors. Defense Department supported research was expedient yet vulnerable to attack by protesting students. Reliance on federal support for research jeopardized institutions when research policy changed as a result of political changes. But eventually some better basis than expediency must be found.

These dilemmas have emerged within a particular context which determined both kind and intensity. There is always the temptation to blame perplexities of such magnitude on the perversity of individuals. And some exacerbation of the conflicts is beyond doubt due to personal weakness. But the widespread confrontation of these dilemmas suggests more impersonal forces than these.

Most significant is the sheer size of higher education and its institutions. When institutions were small and when the total enrollment and cost of American higher education were relatively insignificant, either these problems did not exist or when they did they were not particularly intense. Small institutions made role fulfillment easy because of reinforcement by many well known people. The registrar, dean of students, custodian, operator of the campus store, housemother, fraternity cook, and local tailor all knew most students, and their interactions determined the student's conception of himself. The president, his wife, members of the board, members of local service clubs, and students knew all or most professors, and their interactions performed the same function. Even the largest pre-World War II institutions such as Illinois or Minnesota were so organized that these socializing forces operated, partly because the student body was relatively homogeneous. When total resources for higher education were but a fraction of Gross National Product and when the chief function of institutions was enculturation of a small proportion of high school graduates, ordering of personal or institutional priorities was no significant issue. But when institutions doubled, tripled, or increased tenfold in size, over a brief period of time, socialization in older ways became impossible, and the growth was so rapid that no new ways were created.

The result was feelings of anomie, alienation, depersonalization and the many conflicts those feelings generated. And when universities demonstrated utility as adjuncts to business and government, they were unprepared to accommodate the pressures placed on them. Nor were academics prepared to accept the scrutiny and control which increasing cost of education attracted. A second thread in this contextual fabric is the rapidity of change both in the total society and in institutions themselves. The post-World War II social revolutions have been well described and need only be mentioned. The revolt of colonial peoples, the technological revolution, the revolution in weapons, the worldwide population explosion, the new affluence, and the exponential increase in knowledge all set the stage. But on campuses equally profound and rapid changes happened. Increases in the proportion of high school graduates attending college resulted in heterogeneous student bodies at first, then later in heterogeneous faculties. For example, the academic hegemony of the WASPs was broken during this period. The knowledge explosion destroyed within a twenty year period any possible unity or integrity of the curriculum, and the cafeteria metaphor became a reality. Negro demands for entry into higher education in sequence brought the colleges to the courts, to the mainstream of civil strife, to revised concepts of admission, and finally to radically new concepts of academic work and professorial preparation. Institutions which could once be governed effectively by a president, a few other officers, and a town meeting style of governance found it necessary to change organizational modes twice or three times a decade and each time to create new roles and new role relationships. And traditional styles of teaching had, from 1948 onward, to accommodate or reject first television then tape recordings, then computers, and then a plethora of still other technological devices. Perhaps the most revealing part of the rapidity of change has been in financial support and budgets. Institutions which in 1960 operated on yearly budgets of fifteen million dollars were spending sixty million or more in 1970. To adjust wisely to such changes in fortune taxed all involved.

Then, society itself and its institutions became complex, and colleges and universities had to relate to them in new and central ways. As a base from which to examine this phenomenon, in 1939 the Naval Research Laboratory offered the Carnegie Institute in Washington fifteen hundred dollars to help investigate the power potential of uranium. The offer was refused because the institute did not wish to be contaminated through government subsidy. Since then, big government has grown bigger and higher education has had to learn to relate to every new element from the advisory committee for the Manhattan Project to the Civil Rights Commission and the selection of nominees for the Supreme Court. The growth of Washington based educational and professional associations is just one index of change. A partial list indicates other new complexities, created in fewer than twenty-five years, which have serious implications for higher education: the creation of the Ford Foundation, the increase in resources of other foundations, the evolution of statewide coordinating committees for higher education, the growth of corporate giving to higher education, the evolution of research based industry relying on universities for expertise, the mergers of educationally oriented companies with the largest corporations of American industry, the creation of large separate research institutes, and the perfection of the jet airliner, which makes the close relationships possible. There is no need to elaborate the moral dilemmas of higher education for each of these. Just consider the impact on one institution and its faculty and students of heavy defense spending, major centers of excellence grants from the Ford Foundation and the National Science Foundation, and the addition to the campus of a 115 million dollar federal research installation— all within fifteen years.

Of a different order is the breakdown in political consensus in the United States, precipitated by the war in Viet Nam, manifested by a loss of faith in the federal government, but actually reflecting a changed world order. Immanuel Wallerstein[1] theorized that from the nineteenth century on world order was in part preserved by one major power which acted in general on liberal principles. First,

[1] I. Wallerstein, *University in Turmoil* (New York: Atheneum, 1969).

131

this power was England and then, from 1914 onward, the United States. Most elements within those nations including the universities supported government efforts to maintain hegemony and to resist threats from other nations even when resistance led to war. After World War II the Soviet Union appeared as a new threat, and in Great Britain, France, and the United States came a crystallization of public opinion slightly to the right of center. This combination was able to wean large numbers of people from the left in opposition to Russia. This situation could normally have been expected to precipitate a move from a cold to a hot war, with the support of even the intellectual community. (Academics were, it should be pointed out, quite ready to share in the national defense effort.) But instead Russia and the Western powers moved toward a detente which resulted in vast disillusionment within the Western intellectual community. As the Cold War ended intellectuals seemed to be saying the following:

> We have been duped. For twenty years you, our governments, . . . have asked us to do many distasteful things, to suppress many moralistic qualms in the interests of the primacy of the moral struggle between the Western and Soviet worlds. All of a sudden there is a detente and you, our government, believe that the "enemy" is not a devil but a force to be bargained with and even cooperated with. And yet you, our government, persist in the distasteful practices without any longer the plausible excuses of the overriding moral-political demands of the "crusade."[2]

Thus intellectuals and the university community were torn from close relationships with government and were torn within themselves when those relationships persisted.

An equally fundamental change was what Walter Metzger has called the delocalization of institutions.[3] Institutions of higher education have lost their isolation and their ability to decide things for themselves. As universities were engulfed by the central city land

[2] *Ibid.*, p. 23.
[3] W. Metzger and others, "Academic Freedom in Delocalized Institutions." In *Dimensions of Academic Freedom* (Urbana, Ill.: University of Illinois Press, 1969).

use became a political issue. Academic innovation derived from bureaucratized philanthropy (private and public). State and federal law affected admissions policy, and state and federal support led to state control exercised through coordinating agencies of various sorts and federal influence exercised through funding policy. Professors no longer looked to the institution for status and reward but rather to New York, Washington, or other sources of finance and influence. Before World War II scholars at even the greatest of research oriented universities had heavy teaching loads and tended to stay home except for the annual trip to one national or regional meeting of a learned society. But as institutions came to look outward, so did their professors, and the flight from teaching became real.

Other elements can be identified. Certainly long held campus values have been challenged and changed. The largest institutions especially have taken on the characteristics of Galbraith's industrial state with the bureaucracy, composed of interchangeable parts, assuming a personality of its own and being in faceless control of institutional destinies. But the search here has been for the most limited set of factors which could explain the critical moral dilemmas.

If these dilemmas are real and if their nature is moral, and if their resolution is imperative for the salvation of the university, a new morality must be contrived. A return to simpler times is not possible. A few individuals may try, but on most campuses and for most of the academic community moral and ethical principles must be evolved which accept and accommodate size, complexity, rapidity of change, and delocalization of all social institutions, not just the university. However, before a new academic morality can be fashioned, some conditions are essential. To create them is no simple task, yet there should be within higher education the capacity to try to do so.

First among these conditions is a legitimate system of governance. Morality cannot exist when no agency is generally accepted as the legitimate authority, for without such a force, individual desires determine behavior unless modified by the forceful or violent

133

expression of the desires of someone else. Much of the confusion on the campus during the 1960s came about because the legitimacy of presidents and boards of trustees was challenged, yet their challengers—first students and then faculty—were unable to achieve legitimacy themselves. Elements such as departments do maintain a legitimacy and a loyalty, but such feudalism is as disruptive to the contemporary university as was medieval feudalism to the emerging nation-state. As to which element may best restore legitimate governance, there can be considerable question. Some feel that a collegiate version of a constitutional monarch may be necessary, while others believe that the abstraction of shared responsibility may yet achieve general acceptance. The only point here is that legitimacy of governance is the only alternative to campus anarchy.

Then a new academic morality will require generally accepted goals of education. As long as there is widespread disagreement over whether the university should be an agency to train professionals, should reform society, or should become the new secular church, acceptable canons of behavior will not be found. Although people on individual campuses find reaching agreement on institutional goals and objectives a time consuming, frequently boring exercise, nonetheless the most viable and influential institutions are those in which there is general awareness and acceptance of where the institution is heading. Some may contend that institutions have become so complex that only an uneasy pluralism is possible. But pluralism is viable in complex systems only if there are commonly shared values and goals, exemplified in a group or agency which can mediate among differing groups. American civilization has succeeded to the degree it has as a pluralistic society because the established, white, Anglo-Saxon, Protestant set of values was pervasive and because representatives of the establishment were able to mediate the views of those who held other beliefs. Peter Schrag pointed out that it is inconceivable that America could ever be integrated on ethnic or other minority terms. John Lindsay, a WASP, was reelected mayor of New York in 1969 because, although the Jews and Negroes may have distrusted him, they trusted Italians even less. In the microcosm of higher education the search must be made for generally accepted basic values which alone can allow some degree of desirable pluralism.

To achieve acceptance of common goals and objectives will require a mediating force on the campus. Again Schrag makes the point with respect to the entire society. "What held the [democratic] world together was not just a belief in some standardized version of textbook Americanism, a catalog of accepted values, but a particular class of people and institutions that we identified with our vision of the country. The people were white and Protestant; the institutions were English; American culture was WASP."[4] Very likely representatives of that same class gave the pre-World War II collegiate institution its integrity. And some version of a similar class must be found again, not necessarily of the same composition but capable of exemplifying a commonly held vision of reality.

The underlying elitism of such a conception of a mediating force is tolerable only if there are well developed, varied, and widely used channels of communication on the campus by which the many minorities—blacks, whites, scientists, engineers, women, deans, educationists, classicists—may express their views and feel that someone is listening. A root problem in complex institutions has been either that these channels did not exist—it was impossible to get word to the president—or that there was no way of knowing whether anyone heard. Feeling powerless to communicate in established ways, people on the campus took to unorthodox methods. Some of the demands of militant students for an open forum with boards of trustees in essence say, "There are no other channels other than confrontation." As channels are opened, there should come a lessening of volume because messages can get through without shouting. And with diminished volume should come a restoration of rationality in discussion, which also seems essential for a new morality.

Another condition is a new system of enculturation of

[4] P. Schrag, "The Decline of the WASP." *Harper's*, 1970, *240* (1439), 85–89.

faculty, students, presidents, board members, and all others on the campus so that role fulfillment can be facilitated. As was previously noted, in earlier and quieter times, professors learned their roles through long tenure and slow advance in one or two institutions. Similarly, students, through parental suggestion or the behavior of college attending sisters, brothers, or friends, learned what it was like to be college students. Those times are, of course, gone. Many now entering college are the first of their family or even community to enter higher education. And this development is to the good. But devices are needed to socialize the millions entering colleges and universities into the peculiar life of academe.

A last essential condition for a new academic morality is inadequately described as a restoration of institutional and professional modesty. In a sense higher education has asked for greater numbers of students, greater amounts and variety of contract research, and greater public scrutiny because its leaders have claimed so much. Expansion of higher education is urged because of the economic benefits it confers on regions and individuals. Higher education is described as the pivotal component in a complex society or as the modern church. Education is proclaimed as the chief instrument of public policy and through it the most critical of domestic problems are to be solved. Higher education claims the right to be the critic as well as the catechist of the entire society, and professors, once a modest breed, have presumed, through this claim, to speak with authority on social and political issues for which their limited expertise does not qualify them. When government, organized philanthropy, business, and the American people took these claims seriously, colleges and universities proved inadequate to the tasks. Higher education has not been able to solve the problems of accepting minority group students, a much less difficult problem than those of urban blight and the ghetto. Journalists, artists outside the academy, and students have been much more astute about and attuned to critical issues in the national life than have college faculties and administrators, whose comments have all too frequently trailed events. These observations are not to deny high significance to higher education. It is an important institution which in limited ways is essential to the nation. But the stridency of past claims should be muted somewhat so that accurate criteria of behavior can be suggested.

Given such a revised context, it is now proper to ask what would be the dimensions of a new academic morality. There should be clear definition and recognition of the public and private roles of people on the campus. As private persons students and faculty have the right to protest through demonstration, to engage if they will in civil disobedience, or to espouse unpopular causes. Whether students sleep all day, drink all night, believe or disbelieve in God, or enjoy an active premarital sex life, and whether professors are Catholic or communist, have chaste or promiscuous sex lives, or favor or oppose the war in Viet Nam are of no concern to their colleges or universities as educational institutions, as long as the students and professors do not claim academic privilege or academic prestige to do so. When students seek to extend freedom over their private lives to freedom over their academic lives or when professors invoke academic freedom as a shield for acts against the campus or the use of classrooms to organize political action, they are as much in violation of academic ethics or morality as is a board of regents which discharges a professor because he is a communist. When professors use the prestige of their academic titles or affiliations to persuade on subjects outside their fields of competence, they are as much in violation of academic morality and freedom as is the institution which violates due process to terminate their appointments.

Then there should also be general acceptance that there are behaviors, techniques, and strategies inappropriate for academic performance, even though they are quite acceptable for other activities. When the professor of public administration begins to take direct political action, he is no longer performing as an academician but as a politician. When students organize campus protest, they are no longer students but private citizens, and academic credit should probably not be allowed, although the protest may very well contribute to personal development. Colleges and universities are designed to provide some kinds of experience which contribute to some kinds of human development. Very likely the list of appropriate experiences is much longer than those generally provided. But the list is still finite, and its limits should be understood. Similarly, research and scholarship are activities which make use of many different techniques, strategies, and approaches. And once again the list of those appropriate is larger than those generally used. But again the list is finite, and its limits should be understood.

There should also be general acceptance that colleges and universities exist to provide a limited number of services to the society, which supports them with limited resources. Although from time to time social demand changes and institutions may change activities—land grant colleges entered agricultural experimentation when American society demanded it and supported it—nevertheless the range is always finite, and the specific services offered should be evaluated in the light of institutional traditions, resources, and capabilities. To be quite specific the nature of the university and of the people who work there suggests that universities should not engage in big science but should leave that to the separate research institute. Health services, counseling, and remedial work are all appropriate activities for a college or university if they are limited to removing relatively superficial barriers to student progress toward academic goals. Housing, religious counseling, and bookstores also can be provided by institutions as long as there is a direct relationship between the service and the academic goals of students and faculty. To attempt more is to invite the sorts of moral dilemmas which have plagued collegiate institutions. If a choice had to be made between expanding peripheral services or eliminating them completely, institutions would be on safer ground to eliminate them, saying in effect to students, "You may come to the university, use its academic resources for your own development, but everything else is your own affair."

Reflecting on the moral dilemmas present on the campus, the forces which produced them, and the conditions which seem necessary if they are to be resolved, I find that the overarching element of a new academic morality is parsimony. Through economy in the use of means to ends, arrogance on the campus may fade, problems of governance may be solved, and the public backlash to higher education may be relieved.

# EPILOGUE

# *Events of May*

Perhaps if students, faculty, indeed all of society could find a new morality, students would not be killed at Jackson State and Kent State; distrust of universities, the government, and each other would not be so prevalent; and democratic and scholarly virtues could once again prevail. Much, if indeed not most, of campus unrest, protest, and violence in the United States during the decade of the sixties is explained by looking at the factors, forces, and failures on the campus itself. True, problems of the larger society intruded on the campus and provided the context and focus for dissent. But external stimulation

140

to campus unrest could have been blunted had the collegiate house not been divided against itself. However, in the spring of 1970, college and university campuses exploded in the most sustained protest yet. It precipitated, or at least contributed to, the most serious national constitutional crisis since the outbreak of the Civil War. The question is, although it is much too early to answer it accurately, Can that spasm be explained as just one more manifestation of earlier campus imbalances or does it require a more fundamental interpretation?

The events can be quickly chronicled. During the summer of 1969 the most extreme radical groups fell apart leaving relatively ineffective splinters. Black students no longer made common cause with radical whites. The several factions of the Students for a Democratic Society split doctrinaire hairs, which led to irrepressible conflict among themselves and left the leadership of the vast majority of students to moderates who believed the system could work. Faculty and administration hoped and believed that the worst was over. They had brought about some educational reforms, accepted students into their councils, and contrived ways to deal with protest which would at the same time safeguard individual rights and institutional vitality and integrity. Although no golden age, the fall and winter months of 1969 and 1970 saw voices muted, the sharpness of the Viet Nam issue blunted, and no radical focus on any other issue sharp enough to attract widespread student support. The first and only important war mobilization protest in October was moderate in tone and effect. Students talked of the ecological crisis and the population bomb, but their revolutionary spirits declined almost in unison with the stock market. Even a bona fide issue such as that of Angela Davis,[1] which seemed destined to bring the faculty of the University of California and its Board of Regents into collision, found its way into the courts instead.

---

[1] Angela Davis, a young, black, female instructor of philosophy at the University of California, Los Angeles, was denied reappointment on the ground that she was a Communist Party member. The case was decided in the courts, and although she was not reappointed, the regents used different reasons, which also will be tested by judicial review.

## Arrogance on Campus

In the early spring small groups of students on a number of campuses did launch crusades against ROTC and made raids on ROTC facilities which were of considerable nastiness, moderately damaging, and of little significance. There were, of course, substantial exceptions, such as the burning of the student union at Kansas. But for the most part these small groups (50 to 150) were being contained, and the damage wrought to university resources and integrity was being kept to tolerable limits.

Then, the tempo quickened. High political figures using intemperate, inaccurate, and inflammatory rhetoric declared, if not war, certainly an end to peace with students. A governor called for a blood bath, the Vice-President of the United States demanded the firing of the president of a private university, and the wife of a cabinet officer, in Marie Antoinette style, dismissed students as just rabble. Throughout the land a faint air of planned repression became detectable, manifested by a seeming conspiracy to destroy the Black Panthers and by a Chicago judge, goaded and irritated no doubt, who sentenced out of personal spite rather than judicial calm and restraint. As though to give cavalier point to the changed climate, the President of the United States, in an act some see as comparable to the Stamp or Tea Acts of earlier times, announced the invasion of Cambodia in rhetoric almost identical to what he had used almost twenty years earlier as Vice-President to condone the anticipated war in Viet Nam. And as Lexington and Concord followed the Intolerable Acts of the British crown, so did Kent State and then Jackson State become the scenes of violence and death.

The national response followed quickly. Campus strife flared, political leaders talked of impeachment and curtailment of presidential funds, and the stock market plunged. The *New York Times* evidenced the gravity and the national significance of the campus by publishing pictures of three university presidents on the front page for the first time in years. (The irony is that three weeks earlier, when another university president issued a major civil rights report, that story and his picture were on page four.) Students threatened to bring great institutions to a complete halt, and college presidents not known for anxiety announced they probably could.

# Events of May

Federal officials did much they had previously announced they never would. The President of the United States finally paid attention to a student strike and even talked to some strikers, his key cabinet members announced definite dates for complete withdrawal of troops from Viet Nam, and a university president became a presidential advisor on the problems of the campus.

None of the events which contributed to this rapid escalation of campus and national strife is unique. Similar events have happened before. Joseph McCarthy helped create a mood of repression in the 1950s. In the 1930s peace movement students clashed with ROTC cadets and vowed never to support their country in war. From the 1940s the constitutional issue over the sale of fifty warships to the British seems similar to that of sending troops into Cambodia, and the issue was not even raised when an earlier Roosevelt sent the Great White Fleet around the world in defiance of Congress. And, of course, killing students on campus was earlier witnessed in the South. But in the spring of 1970 the constellation of events split the national fabric, and the question must be raised as to why. Only by answering the question wisely can we contribute to a restoration of tranquility. Until ultimate answers are provided, several hypotheses can be examined and, if even partially valid, can be used to bring about change.

First among these is the theory of a bumbling generation and an accretion of error which brought results no one wanted. The American Civil War and World War II were in large measure brought on because men of too limited vision failed to consider available alternatives and became captive to uncontrolled events precipitated through error. In the spring of 1970 the American President seemingly failed to consider the full ramifications of a new military move, college and university presidents failed to consider the inflammatory effects of statements sympathetic to radical students, high political figures used rhetoric without thought of consequences, students sought to close down institutions which once closed could never recover losses in people and finances, and faculty members polarized themselves over issues without thought for institutional well being. In aggregate these errors produced what no

143

one could have anticipated. The White House aide who told the Secretary of the Interior to "cool it because the fuss will be over in twenty-four hours" only illustrates the shocked surprise of the entire nation.

A second hypothesis is that the American Constitution is no longer a sufficient document for a postindustrial society in the military age of the atomic bomb. Constitutional limitation of powers is a doctrine evolved in a much simpler time and can no longer contain an executive branch forced to deal quickly with events spotlighted before the world by instant television. This theory holds that people have been subconsciously aware of constitutional weakness but unwilling to face the reality of it, for the stability of other institutions—business, the family, the economic community, and education—rested on a faith in constitutionalism. When an event revealed that the system of checks and balances had failed and that powers of the legislative branch had been assumed by the executive, the legitimacy of every other institution was brought into question. And when the constitutional crisis followed so closely examples of misuse of police power, official misinformation of the public, and official castigation of other legitimate social institutions such as the press, people had apocalyptic visions. Very likely the Constitution is still a workable document and the American government essentially stable. But the thought that it might not be helps explain the turmoil which struck the campuses.

A third theory is that of conspiracy. Although generally conspiracy interpretations of historical events have proven inadequate, they must always be examined. There is the claim that a southern strategy is specifically designed to build a political power base which will exclude Negroes, intellectuals, and those who dwell in the largest cities. Others see the eastern establishment as out to deny the central government the right to govern through control of the press and universities. Still others believe that campus protest stems directly from a communist plot or at least from a plot of a small group of radical leaders who have organized each major upset. There is the tenet of militant black people that there is a pervasive white conspiracy to deny blacks not only entry into the mainstream of society but their very existence. To these fears should be added the thesis that universities, industry, and the military have deliberately created a closed corporation, which for self-preservation and profits would deny the people the right to a peaceful world or the belief that a military-industrial complex has gained hegemony over the society. Most of these theses can be exploded through careful analysis, but the fact that so many see conspiracy creates a climate of suspicion which intensifies even relatively minor events. In such a climate otherwise rational people can see deliberate intent behind the shooting of students at Kent State or the claim of the governor of California that there should be a blood bath.

Of a different order is the concept that in every society there are significant divisions among different groups of people, some potentially destructive. But a stable society develops ways of accommodating differences, short of violence. Thus in the United States the traditional cleavages along religious, economic, regional, political, and even racial lines have been so institutionalized that limits of expression of mutual opposition have been generally recognized. However, beginning in the early 1960s new fractionalization of the society began along completely new lines. Some of these lines were close to older splits. Within the Negro community the influence of moderate leadership trying to work for assimilation into the mainstream of the society weakened, and black power and black separatism emerged as an uncontrolled division. However, other divisions were new. The children of the intellectual and professional middle classes began their revolt against that class and the society which had nurtured them. Following closely was an ideological affinity between the previously antagonistic blue collar worker and management over such matters as political party, quest for law and order, and attitude toward the war in Viet Nam. The uneasy coalition which elected Nixon is a manifestation of this detente. And, precipitated by concerns over the war and the exacerbating comments of political leadership, a serious fault has developed within the national establishment itself. Thus, the president of Yale attacked the courts, other university presidents used the prestige of their high offices to criticize government policy they had supported half a decade earlier, and professors and their students made common cause against their institutions. These new social divisions are explosive because established roles of opposition have not been achieved, limits to opposition behavior have not been accepted, limits to reaction have not been drawn, and channels for nondestructive release of tensions have not been created. Thus, university presidents do not know how to react to personal attack by the Vice-President of the United States. Universities have been as unsure how to deal with the violence of their students as are middle class parents whose children suddenly declare them to be enemies. Until limits to violence and constraints to opposition are accepted, every confrontation between these new oppositions can expand and precipitate a fibrillating campus or society.

Each of these hypotheses seems partially valid, and in aggregate they might be sufficient to explain the national and campus crisis, particularly after a decade of marked arrogance on campus. A people suddenly divided along new and little understood lines, anxious over the stability of their basic political institution, mutually suspicious because of charges and countercharges of conspiracy, and provided inept leadership is vulnerable to revolutionary disruption. Thus, when unexpected expansion of the war and death on the campus struck, every segment and every institution of society was quickly affected.

Obviously the hypotheses do not settle the more fundamental question of why—why a constitutional failure, why conspiracy, why new social cleavages, or why consistent gross error in judgment. Underlying these critical issues, however, are several themes, the origins of which are difficult to discover, but the significance of which is enormous. The first of these is simply a pronounced, pervasive loss of trust or credibility. Colleges and universities claimed to be able to do too much and when they failed to perform as expected the wider public lost faith in them. The young lost faith in the older generation for many reasons but mostly because it claimed too much and failed. The good material life did not produce happiness, elaborate defenses did not preclude war, and

**146**

neither the new frontier nor Texas populism yielded a just life. Thus, everything said by elders became suspect. Then, the entire society began to suspect its government. Presidential statements and official reports seemed to conceal more than they revealed. Suspicion cast alike on the Warren Commission or on battle reports led to a general assumption that something was always being covered up. Added to this, of course, was the eroding credibility concerning established professions. Medical doctors were judged more concerned about fees than health, lawyers as being unconcerned about human rights, and professors and teachers as being chiefly interested in becoming members of another affluent profession. Despite press agentry, police came to be mistrusted pigs, military officers at best corrupt and at worst murderers, and the corporate world willing to sacrifice human life and safety for profit. Above all ancient values seemed to have lost meaning and trust, and newer values were judged the same way. God died, nice girls did, the Bill of Rights was a communist plot, and the Constitution was a tool of the establishment.

In search for relief from the anxiety which distrust provoked, people turned to romanticism. Perhaps if formal institutions and rational behavior could not be trusted, feeling and emotion could. Fantasy from drugs was better than painful awareness of rational hypocrisy, and if the establishment was depraved primitive people and practice might not be. Since material goods brought so little happiness a return to nature might yield more. It should be noted that romanticism was embraced by the political left and right. Max Rafferty's quest for old time virtue is the same phenomenon as the quest of flower children for contentment. And Agnew's distrust of the press and intellectuals is the same distrust as that of the advocates of participatory democracy. What makes the current variety of romanticism so dangerous is that it has been joined by an intensified faith in violence. Violence has generally been used in controlled and constrained ways by the established order to maintain its sway; its use is limited by at least quasirational considerations. But so deep has become public disenchantment with rationality that the use of violence to overcome it seems defensible. And violence governed by feeling and emotion knows no bounds and accepts no limitations. Thus, the burning of buildings or the use of military power to defend a mystical national honor results from romanticism in search of absolute truth. Violent rejection of ROTC in hopes its abolishment would end war and political appeal to a silent majority to support violence seem equally antirational behaviors.

Widespread mutual mistrust and romanticism which turned violent when coupled with a widespread sense of powerlessness seem sufficient to explain the impasse in the 1970s. American institutions are so big, the faceless bureaucracy so insensitive, and the problems of war, racism, and pollution so enormous that people are left feeling life is uncontrolled and uncontrollable. In many respects the outbursts on the campus in May 1970 exemplified this feeling exactly. The longest war in the nation's history seemed about to be prolonged by a faceless military bureaucracy persuading a distrusted political leader to act regardless of the consequences. Student response was romantic and became violent, as was official reaction.

As to the future, several courses seem open. If the events of May follow the pattern of other revolutionary and reforming movements, reaction and repression will follow. Student protests in Russia, Germany, Serbia, and France during the nineteenth century were all followed by harsh repression and a weakening of constitutional safeguards for human well-being. And there are signs that official repression is building up in the United States. The chancellor of the Ohio system warned on the day following the killings at Kent State that he expected legislative restrictions. The governor in California and the boards of the state colleges and the university seem bent on curtailing campus freedoms. But this repression need not happen.

Already student groups seem to have decided not to take an extreme course but rather to try once again to work somewhat within the existing political system. The President and the Congress seem to be trying to avoid a true constitutional crisis. Faculty members, even quite militant ones, seem to have recoiled from the stand that closing institutions was quite tolerable for the sake of ideal principles. If these tendencies continue, breathing time may be allowed for creating new systems of education, of governance, and of democratic life. The essence of the American system is compromise arrived at through time. Perhaps that spirit of compromise may again prevail.

# *Index*

**151**

# Index

Alumni, 111

American Association for Higher Education (AAHE), 65, 68, 100

American Association of University Professors (AAUP), 65, 68, 70, 74, 81, 95, 104, 105, 108

American Federation of Teachers (AFT), 65–66, 68, 102

Antioch College, 39, 56

Appointments, 60, 61, 90, 103

Arrogance: of administration, 3, 4, 10; and campus unrest, 1–12; of faculty, 3–4, 7–10; of students, 3, 4–7, 10–11; of trustees, 3, 10

ASTEN, A. W., 86

## B

BECKER, H. S., 36

Behaviorism, 8

BENNETT, I. L., 116

Black studies, 4

Block scheduling, 38

Brandeis University, 27, 28

Bureaucracy, 48

## C

Calendars, academic, 37

California, University of, Berkeley, 20, 31, 68, 89, 109, 111

California, University of, Los Angeles, 141

California, University of, Santa Cruz, 38

Cambodian invasion, 142

Campus unrest, 20, 22–23, 28–29, 140–149; and arrogance, 1–12; and conspiracy, 144–145; and faculty, 3–4, 7–10, 28, 87–88; legislation on, 6, 22, 26–27, 148

CANOS, R. J., 86

CAREY, J. T., 19

Carnegie Institute, 131

Catholic University of America, 65

Chicago, University of, 27, 28, 36, 64, 126

Chicago City Junior College, 65

Chicago Teachers College, 38

City University of New York, 68

Classroom Teachers Association, 66

CLEAVER, E., 17, 109

Cluster colleges, 38

Cold War, 132

Columbia University, 20, 31, 36, 67, 83, 87, 97, 126

Confrontation, 5, 16, 28, 30–31, 135; and academic freedom, 97–98, 109; escalation of, 77

Conspiracy, 144–145

Constitution, United States, 144

Constitutionalism, 12, 55–56, 74–75; and administration, 75; and review, 59

Consultants, faculty as, 9–10, 83, 98–99

Contextual courses, 41

Coordinating agencies, 50, 59–60, 68, 96

Cornell University, 3, 28

CORSON, J., 52

Credibility gap, 146–147

Curriculum, 30–46; and career, 35–36; change in, 36–40; contextual courses, 41; and development, 20–21, 32–36; general education, 36–37, 40–42; lecture courses, 43; liberal studies, 41; major concentration, 41; media in, 38, 44; off-campus experiences, 39, 43; primary groups in, 43; and students, 20–21, 48, 60, 111–112

## D

DAVIS, A., 141

Defense research, 5, 31, 49, 64

Delocalization of institutions, 132–133

Development, personal, 61, 120; and curriculum, 20–21, 32–36; student protest as, 34

Discretionary action, 74

Duke University, 31, 87

152

# Index

## E

East-West Center, 54
Educational theory, 116
Elective system, 80
ELIOT, C., 80
Experimental colleges, 38

## F

Faculty, 62–78; academic freedom of, 73, 98–109; and academic revolution, 62, 79–89; and administration, 4, 10, 29, 52–53, 63–64, 65, 67, 68, 73–74, 75, 81, 88–89, 102–103, 108; arrogance of, 3–4, 7–10; and behaviorism, 8; and campus unrest, 3–4, 7–10, 28, 87–88; and change, 3, 37, 80, 86–87; as consultants, 9–10, 83, 98–99; evaluation of, 84, 106–107; and finances, 67, 73, 74, 82, 89, 103; governance by, 9, 50–51, 52–53, 60–61, 67, 73–74, 76, 81, 88; and the institution, 75, 106, 107–108; in legislation, 64, 72; and planning, 28, 29, 74, 75; powers of, 53, 60; and public, 98, 102, 106; research by, 8–9, 64, 70, 84–85, 99; role of, 7–8, 125; salaries of, 66–67, 81, 100–102; senates, 65; strikes by, 65, 66, 101–102, 107; and students, 3, 10, 28, 29, 50–51, 52–53, 60–61, 64, 68, 69–70, 82–85, 86, 98, 106, 112–113, 125, 128; syndicalism of, 53, 70; teaching by, 4, 9, 37, 64, 99, 112; traits of, 7, 63, 69–70, 75–76, 79–80; and trustees, 65, 67, 73, 81; unionism in, 50–51, 63, 65–66, 68, 101–102
FELDMAN, K. A., 86
Finances, 55, 60; and academic freedom, 97, 103; and faculty, 67, 73, 74, 82, 89, 103; and student protest, 6

FLEXNER, A., 80
Florida State University, 38
Ford Foundation, 131
Fractionalization of society, 145–146
FRIEDENBERG, E., 83
FUCHS, R. F., 96

## G

GALBRAITH, J. K., 88, 133
General education, 36–37, 40–42, 80
GIDEONSE, H. D., 113
GILMAN, D. C., 80
GOLDMAN, E., 9–10
GOODMAN, P., 23, 83
Governance: by faculty, 9, 50–51, 52–53, 60–61, 67, 73–74, 76, 81, 88; students in, 47–61; by trustees, 49–50, 53, 60, 73
Graduate education, 80, 91–92, 118, 120–122
Graduate Record Examination, 86
GREELEY, A., 34, 111

## H

Harvard Report, 36
Harvard University, 3, 6, 10, 83
Hawaii, University of, 54
HEFFERLIN, JB L., 86
HESBURGH, T., 22
Higher education, 89–92, 110–123, 129–130, 137–139; crisis in, 2–3; finances of, 55, 60, 89; functions of, 52, 110–111, 119–120, 134, 138; governance in, 50–61; growth of, 129–130; planning in, 50, 54; and the public, 51, 80, 98, 116, 118; and society, 113–114, 128–129, 138; and student protest, 3–4; successes of, 2
Hofstra College, 38
House plan, 38
Humanities, 8
HUTCHINS, R. M., 80

## I

Illinois, University of, 129
Independent study, 42–43

153

# Index

Institute for Defense Analysis, 31
Institutionalism, 48, 75
Intellectual narcissism, 81
Issue-oriented courses, 39

## J

Jackson State College, 140, 142
JOHNSON, B. L., 87
JOHNSON, L. B., 10
Judicial system, 27
Junior College Faculty Association, 66

## K

KADISH, S. H., 72, 101
KATZ, J., 33, 86, 111
KENISTON, K., 111
Kent State University, 140, 142, 148
KING, M. L., JR., 31, 114

## L

Lecture courses, 43
Legislation, 137–138; and academic freedom, 94–97; on campus unrest, 6, 22, 26–27, 148; faculty in, 64, 72; and student protest, 6; and tenure, 95
Legitimacy, 133–134
LEVENSON, E. A., 19
Liberal studies, 41
LINDSAY, J., 134
LUNDSTEDT, S., 116

## M

MC CARTHY, J., 144
MC CONNELL, T. R., 106
MC EVOY, J., 87
Machiavellianism, 103–104
Major concentration, 41
MARTIN, W., 86
Materialism, 11
Media, 38, 44, 115
Medical education, 80
MEDSKER, L. L., 111
METZGER, W. P., 94, 132
Michigan State University, 38
MILLETT, J., 99

Minnesota, University of, 129
MITCHELL, M., 142
MUTTER, A., 87

## N

National Education Association (NEA), 66, 68
Negroes: admissions of, 114–115; and militance, 17; and racism, 17–18
NEWCOMB, T. M., 86
NIXON, R. M., 22, 142
Northeastern University, 39
Notre Dame, University of, 22

## O

Off-campus experiences, 39, 43
Overseas programs, 39–40

## P

Pacific, University of the, 38
Participatory democracy, 16, 25, 55
Pedantry, 80
Perfectibility of man, 11
Personal freedom: and academic morality, 137; of students, 21–22, 48, 49, 61
Pittsburgh, University of, 37
Planning: and faculty, 28, 29, 74, 75; students in, 28–29, 50, 54
Police on campus, 10, 22, 28–29
Pragmatism, 11
Primary groups, 43, 56–57
Public: and faculty, 98, 102, 106; and higher education, 51, 80, 98, 116, 118; vs. students, 22–23, 51

## R

Racism, 17–18
RAFFERTY, M., 97, 147
REAGAN, R., 6, 96, 142
Regrouping, educational, 38–39
Research, 114, 117–118, 120–122; by faculty, 8–9, 64, 70, 84–85, 99; vs. teaching, 9, 64, 117–118, 121
Review of decisions, 59

154

# Index

155